T0036988

INVERSE
COWGIRL

INVERSE
COWGIRL

a memoir

ALICIA
ROTH
WEIGEL

Foreword by
Jonathan Van Ness

HARPERONE

An Imprint of HarperCollins*Publishers*

HarperCollins books may be purchased for educational, business, or sales promotional use. For information, please email the Special Markets Department at SPsales@harpercollins.com.

FIRST EDITION

Illustrations © Jonathan Bush

Library of Congress Cataloging-in-Publication Data has been applied for.

ISBN 978-0-06-329528-5

23 24 25 26 27 LBC 5 4 3 2 1

AUTHOR'S NOTE

This is a work of nonfiction. The tales are all true and each experience has been faithfully rendered as I remember it, to the best of my ability. Not all conversations that made it into these pages are written to represent word-for-word documentation; rather, I've retold some of them in a way that evokes the real feeling and meaning of what was said, in keeping with the true spirit of the interaction and the people involved. A few names and identities have been changed—from adolescent queen bees to that guy who sent me unsolicited flowers—and some circumstances were tweaked in order to protect the integrity and/or anonymity of the individuals involved. (Despite the variety of creative names I give her on a daily basis, my dog is in fact called Chiquita, and when I reference Bad Bunny, I mean business...)

I dedicate this book to intersex kids, of all ages (and Bad Bunny)

CONTENTS

Contents

FOREWORD

Alicia Roth Weigel is one of the most brilliant thought leaders I have been able to share space with. In the summer of 2021 I was privileged to meet Alicia for the first time at a JVN Hair event, and, lucky for me, Alicia was waiting to introduce herself, and thus our friendship happened quite immediately thereafter.

Alicia's work is informed by her life experiences. Her ability to speak to those experiences—boldly, candidly, and publicly—has been incredible to witness. *Inverse Cowgirl* contains vital information for everyone who is seeking to unseat the power of the patriarchal binary that continues its destructive path through society.

In order for us to dismantle the violence the gender binary produces, we must first understand the myriad of ways that it works in society. In our society, no group of people is more often left out of the conversation than our intersex siblings. Intersex people are immediately subjected to medical, emotional, and complex mental challenges that their cisgender peers are not. Intersex people and their families face a daunting path where they must navigate between needing continued medical intervention throughout their lives, but also trying to avoid public ridicule. Biological sex is not binary and intersex people are the embodied proof of this. Yet intersex people are simultaneously under-represented in LGBTQIA activist circles, and their platforms are very infrequently given mainstream media coverage.

A lack of access to healthcare, toxic masculinity, sexual violence, domestic violence, the gender wealth gap, the gender pay gap, poverty, transphobia, homophobia, toxic misogyny–all of these ills originate from our view of the modern-day gender binary. Alicia's work lays out in clear detail why this is the case and what we can do to stop it.

Alicia's work is brave, unflinching, and joyful at the same time. Seeing someone so clearly know who they are and use their knowledge to make the world a better place for others is what I think life is really about–taking one's pain and turning that into purpose. *Inverse Cowgirl* is an incredible piece of work that we are so lucky to witness and marks the beginning of a career that we are all so grateful to observe. Alicia's voice, storytelling, and all-out bravery shine through this piece of literature, and I am incredibly grateful that it has found its way to you.

Jonathan Van Ness

PREFACE

I started writing this book the week that half of the United States lost the rights to their own bodies. These are rights I never had in the first place, even before the reversal of *Roe v. Wade*—but we'll get to that. I wrote this decidedly progressive memoir all over a "deeply red" state. My literary journey kicked off in far West Texas, nestled in the beautiful Davis Mountains that separate Marfa from El Paso. It ended in Round Top, a small town in the cow country that lies between Houston and the capital city. Inverse cowgirls like me live all over the Lone Star State, not just in liberal havens like Austin. Intersex people, in fact, span not just the entire South, but approximately 150 million of us live across the country and around the world. This book is a testament to that fact. I look forward to bringing y'all along for the ride.

You may be wondering what intersex means. I'm not surprised. Though statistically we're as common as redheads (about 2 percent of the world's population), our identity is erased not just from history books but even in the present day. We are present in society but hidden in plain sight. Yes, the *I* in LGBTQIA+ is for "intersex," but as of now, it might as well stand for "invisible." We're not exotic, but we are exhausted—constantly struggling for recognition or mere acknowledgment of our existence. Our identity is stuck in the shadows, and I hope this book might shed some light on why. But instead of giving a hypermedicalized, diagnostic definition of intersex as you might find on the internet, I'd rather share my story in order to *show* you what intersex truly means—not just what doctors try to tell us it means. You'll get a sense of not just *what* we are but *who* we are.

To start at the beginning, we have to rewind just over three decades, a bit before I was born...

When my mom was pregnant with me, she and my father got into a fender bender. After they were rushed to the hospital, doctors performed an amniocentesis test to check on the fetus, or zygote, or whatever phase cluster of cells I was at that point, to ensure that the crash had not terminated the pregnancy. The test told my parents that I'd be fine and that I had XY chromosomes, so they prepared for the arrival of a baby boy. They painted the nursery walls blue and decided on the name Charles, after my father and both my grandfathers. Needless to say, when I came out of the womb with a vagina, everyone was pretty confused. My parents were now experiencing a gender fender bender (shout-out to the activist and artist Mari Wrobi for coining that term). They hadn't picked any "girl" names, but once my father recovered from nearly fainting after my birth—he doesn't do well with blood—he voiced an idea: "We could name her Alicia. I've always liked the name since that hurricane hit when we lived in Houston." Thus, a force of nature was born.

Because the doctors were certain that my genotype was at odds with my physicality—"girl" genitalia with "boy" chromosomes—they knew something was up from the moment I left my mom's birth canal. All humans actually start out with a common genital anatomy until seven weeks after conception, when they then sexually differentiate. Some intersex folks like me stop there and end up somewhere in between the sexes, hence inter-sex—though that word was never used in my delivery room. They notified my parents that I had a "disorder of sexual development" (DSD) called complete androgen insensitivity syndrome (CAIS). Despite my XY genetic blueprint, my sexual development had been arrested in the womb. My clitoris didn't turn into a phallus, and my testes remained internal; I also didn't come with ovaries or a uterus to potentially house my own kid one day—my first shortcoming as a human being.

As we know, society places women's worth in their ability to bear children. Fertility is the perceived pinnacle of our existence and what marks us as female. Because of my external anatomy, they ticked the "F" box on my birth certificate—there still is no available option on this document for intersex people, born in between—but from my first breaths I was seen as a defective female, a girl who needed to be "fixed."

Despite the fact that my testes would eventually produce testosterone and that I would pee some of it out, while naturally converting most of the rest to estrogen, they were seen as the wrong organs for my body. The way I see it, the ability to convert hormones like that is a superpower. I could have worn my baby blanket like a superhero cape, but unfortunately, the world doesn't yet view it that way. My body didn't fit on the prescribed piece of paper needed to render my existence in the world as valid, so rather than adjusting the piece of paper, doctors "adjusted" my body...

Within the first year of my life, I underwent a gonadectomy—in normal speak, they castrated me. Euphemisms are helpful when trying to mask eugenics as necessary medical practice—in this case, referring to a forced sterilization as a "needed" surgery. The decision to perform this surgery was based on incomplete information the doctors fed my parents, claiming that my testes could become cancerous one day—technically not untrue, as any organ in anyone's body theoretically could. But when a parent hears the C word, their natural instinct is to do whatever is in their power to protect their child from harm. Unfortunately, what doctors *didn't* share with my parents is that my risk of developing testicular cancer in the distant future was only between 1 and 5 percent. Certainly no one is out there sterilizing all male infants motivated by a slim chance of testicular cancer one day (though after the Supreme Court's decision about *Roe* in 2022, many women might advocate for reconsidering that).

I know my parents feel a lot of guilt for having made certain decisions for me that weren't necessarily in my best interest. I imagine many other parents of intersex kids feel the same. When I first came out as intersex and started to advocate for my community, my mom and dad felt I was advocating against them. This ultimately led to a chasm in our relationship, and we didn't speak for the better portion of a year before my mom came around—through considerable therapy-led introspection—and became a

staunch advocate for intersex people. I felt a lot of guilt throughout this period; I believed I was a "bad daughter," causing strife
in my family to live my own best life. But I had decided that after
a quarter-century of living by rules they and my doctors had im-
posed on me, it was time to write my own. This gut-wrenching
decision is one many in our LGBTQIA+ community have had
to make—choosing our own joy over the safety of the status quo.
Guilt is rooted in shame, though, and this book is a shame-free
space. These pages are dedicated to real accountability.

Speaking of, I feel compelled to apologize in advance. I feel
remorse for sharing certain things here that stems from a desire
to shield some friends and family members from harm, despite
the fact that they didn't always shield me in return. As an activist working to change systems, I often have to expose individual actors within them—people who lead very private lives that
they'd never opt to having a bunch of strangers read about. How
I portray others in these pages might ultimately destroy my relationships with them. I hope not, but the path to accountability
is always messy; sometimes there are casualties along the way.
The only way to ensure you make it through the darkness and
arrive at that destination is a commitment to be guided solely by
the light of truth, harsh and unforgiving as it often is. Besides the
hurricane that led to my moniker, Alicia apparently also means
"truthful" in a variety of cultures; in a way, my parents set me up
for this path, and I'm just living up to my name.

It is hard, though—as an imperfect person—to examine your
life with as much honesty and integrity as possible, knowing
that your story also involves and sometimes implicates other

imperfect people, who maybe haven't met themselves as deeply as you have yet. I believe, however, in the potential for any human being to heal, grow, and change, regardless of how entrenched certain patterns may be. There'd be no point to devoting years of my life to building movements—or to dedicating many months' worth of nights and weekends to pouring my soul into these pages—if I didn't. So, to paraphrase Eminem, sorry Mama, but tonight I'm cleanin' out my closet.

But let's hop out of the closet and back into the operating room: The doctors and my parents decided early on to cut out the parts of me that didn't fit the female mold. They took my testes and, in doing so, launched me into future hormone withdrawal. Maybe they weren't the "proper" hormone-producing organs for a "lady" to have, but they would have played a vital role in regulating my bodily functions and keeping me healthy. Taking my testes out meant I would have to rely on hormone replacement therapy (HRT) for the rest of my life—a choice some trans folks make for themselves but that I didn't have an opportunity to weigh in on. Living without testes and adequate medical care guiding my HRT over time also eventually leached enough calcium from my bones that I developed osteoporosis in my early thirties. In essence, by trying to fix me, doctors broke me.

I lost control over my reproductive organs at the hands of authority figures who claimed they knew what sort of life I ought to lead. Sound familiar? We intersex people are deemed second-class citizens, without decision-making power over our bodies and the surgical "alterations" made to them. These operations change the trajectory of our health and gender presentation for the rest of our lives but continue to be enacted without our having any say in the process. As author and activist Jennifer Wright tweeted in 2019: "You can't take organs from a corpse without the deceased's written permission, even if it will save lives. When you outlaw abortion, you're allowing women less bodily autonomy than the dead." I replied, twenty-nine years and a day after I was born: "Now's as good a time as ever to remind folks that #Intersex folks have organs ripped from our bodies without our consent on the daily."

My body autonomy died the minute I entered this world. My reproductive rights were stripped from me before I turned a year old, when they took from me my germ cells (the founder cells of all sexually reproducing organisms) without asking. Even if they had asked, I was too young to be able to form the words to respond. How do you cry for help when you have no voice? Three decades later, people with wombs across the United States are starting to understand the violation I've felt every day since leaving Pennsylvania Hospital, in the birthplace of our nation, in my mother's arms. Setting aside the whitewashing of history books, I can't think of anything more American than state-sanctioned violence against women and children, really. That's what these surgeries on intersex children are... violence.

Many nations *don't* sanction nonconsensual and medically unnecessary surgeries on intersex kids, from countries like Greece and Kenya, which have banned them, to those like Portugal and Germany, which condemn them. The State of New York has since followed suit on the latter. Three US Surgeons General have called for a moratorium on these operations on children too young to participate in the decision; the World Health Organization opposes this "forced, coercive and otherwise involuntary sterilization"; and the United Nations prohibits intersex genital mutilation—reconstructive operations some intersex folks suffer on their genitalia—by international law, arguing that it meets the criteria for "torture." Yet these surgeries still happen daily in hospitals across the world.

I imagine this all might surprise you. Many societies revere doctors as if they are gods, but they are, in fact, very human. That doesn't stop many of them from attempting to *play* God, determining the physical form of human beings, without their agency, in ways that—as my mom once put it—shouldn't define but often do confine intersex individuals for the rest of our lives. Some of these doctors are well-intentioned but undereducated; I hope this book will help illuminate a better path for them. But there are many who will never see the light, who've heard our cries and continue to hurt us anyway. There are bad actors in every industry, and every system that exists is hamstrung by capitalist greed. The medical-industrial complex is as real as the school-to-prison pipeline; the exploitation of human beings will continue as long as there are profits to be made.

If you stop reading now, I hope you've at least started to see the point. The rest of this book expands upon how a life turns out when folks don't listen to the experts, doctors ignore their Hippocratic oath to do no harm, and people get hurt. It also demonstrates how to reclaim your power when you've been denied adequate healthcare and stripped of the right to decision-making about your own body. I imagine many Americans might find those lessons helpful, now that abortion access is no longer a federal guarantee.

The stories I share each map to one of my ten tattoos, which serve to organize these essays. Getting "branded," to stick with the cowgirl theme, has been for me what psychologists refer to as an embodiment practice—a physical approach to reconnect with my body, when so many intersex folks have learned to dissociate to survive. Per every hypochondriac's favorite resource, WebMD tells us: "Dissociation is a break in how your mind handles information. You may feel disconnected from your thoughts, feelings, memories, and surroundings." Since we intersex people are treated like lab rats by researchers, gawked at by uninformed healthcare professionals like animals in a zoo, and generally lose control over our own physical form as children—when we most need to feel safe to thrive—dissociation is a learned coping mechanism many of us share.

Embodiment is the opposite of dissociation. It's literally bringing myself back into my body. I do this through meditative trail running, yoga, snuggling with my dog, Chiquita, and dancing. I started this last one early, as evidenced by copious home videos of me cutting a rug with my brother, Max, and neighbor since age two, Artemis. I was always the last one to leave the dance floor at bar and bat mitzvahs and, having discovered Daddy Yankee on Napster or LimeWire around that same time, could often be found *perreando sola* in my bedroom since middle school. (Reggaeton continues to be my refuge; Bad Bunny's music has been particularly healing for me, as it is for so much of the queer community he seeks to lift up through his music.

Perhaps he will one day read this and we can get married—but I digress.)

I also achieve embodiment through my tattoos. A lot of the decisions about what happened to my body or what it would look like were taken away from me as a kid, so getting inked helps me literally own my own skin. Each tat is something that I find beautiful and correlates to a specific phase of my life or facet of my being. I hope that weaving these stories together based on the designs on my skin will help y'all connect the dots on why we intersex people deserve control over our own lives—what our physical appearance looks like and what goes on underneath it. We *all* deserve autonomy over our bodies. While many intersex activists agitate for abortion access, I hope the essays that follow might generate reciprocal support.

Perhaps you found your way here through watching *Every Body*, the Focus Features documentary that includes my work, which also dives into the story of John Money—a Johns Hopkins research doctor who's responsible for a lot of the current medical injustice we face today. I haven't mentioned much medical research here. The goal, rather, is to share real stories to help regain the humanity that's been stripped of us, having been treated as specimens by Dr. Money and others who've followed in his footsteps. His work sufficiently dehumanized us to be able to justify the abuse we face; in a 1963 medical theater, he referred to us as presenting a "strange partial reversal in human beings." I hope through reading this book you'll determine that I am—we are—not so strange. I will not bear the label of a partially reversed human, but I do wear the badge of inverse cowgirl with pride.

This book isn't just for other intersex people, though I do hope they might feel seen in these pages. An inverse cowgirl is anyone whose experience defies the expected and turns societal notions upside down. I'm writing this for everyone who doesn't fit neatly into a box, who's always felt "too" this or "not enough" that. I still wrestle with feeling too intersex to fit in cis-women circles but at the same time too heteronormative to fit into queer spaces. Every human sometimes feels like a lone ranger, but the more we signal our weirdness to the world, the easier it'll be to find one another and feel more at home on the range.

This manifesto isn't a call to think "outside the box"; it's an invitation to dream beyond boxes. We are not outside, or "other." The box doesn't actually exist—we do. Whatever box white supremacy or the cis-heteropatriarchy is trying to shove you in: resist. Intersex bodies are a walking reminder to hold space for the "both/ands" in life. We can be any and all things, all of the time. I'm a city official *and* an underwear model; I wear both of those badges with equal pride.

To anyone who never really "fit" into whatever box the world tried to place you in: congrats, you've won. If it doesn't feel that way yet, consider following along on my journey as a pathway to the winner's circle. I always preferred circles to squares anyway. The unbroken circle on the intersex flag symbolizes wholeness and completeness. Regardless of what any of us has been led to believe—on the basis of our sex, gender, persuasion, race, religion, or whatever other label we carry—we are enough. And that's more than enough editorializing in the abstract when there's a weird and windy road ahead of us. Let's ride...

ORCHID

Like flowers, intersex people are natural, and our
existence is beautiful. Our community, like any garden,
relies on outside help to survive and thrive.

My first childhood crush was on Captain von Trapp in *The Sound
of Music*. We could probably unpack that on a variety of levels . . . yeah, Christopher Plummer was a babe, but it was really
the singing that got me and above all the scene where he rips up
the Nazi flag. I first watched the movie with my paternal grand-
father, Papa, who also fought the Nazis in World War II. My family is of Austrian and German descent—so the scene felt familiar.
And as I've already established, I've held a flame of resistance
inside me since before I was born; antifascist demonstrations just

do it for me. What brings me to tears every time, though, is CvT's rendition of "Edelweiss," a song about a flower that is protected in Austria and illegal to pick or harm. "May you bloom and grow, bloom and grow forever." That part sticks with me.

Flowers are also used to welcome folks in many cultures. As I welcome you into the intersex movement, we'll kick off with another flower—the symbol that unifies our activism: the orchid, which is tattooed on my right shoulder. The word "orchid" comes from the ancient Greek word ὄρχις (órkhis) for "testicle" or "testis"; as so many intersex people have had our testes taken from us like I did, this flower has come to symbolize our fight for wholeness. I can't see the tattoo myself without using a mirror, but I know it's there. It reminds me and others that although our identity isn't always visible, it is ever-present and should not be ignored. It reminds me that I am just a branch of orchids with deep roots planted by intersex activists who struggled before me. And it reminds y'all that intersex people are fighting for the ability to grow—nurtured, yet untouched—and to bloom as who we are.

Yet the surgery I suffered to remove my testes is also sometimes referred to as an orchidectomy. Though I had hand-drawn orchids stamped on my scapula later in life, the doctors removed my *órkhis* from my abdomen in infancy, leaving a small scar. This marks (literally and figuratively) the beginning of a long string of medical interventions that shaped the course of my life, from the physical shape of my body to the soul inside it. The soul is that of a fighter. I like to say that I am literally defiance embodied; I didn't follow the usual development trajectory of my XY genetic blueprint in utero, and I certainly haven't heeded many other arbitrary rules I don't vibe with since.

My mom would say that I've always been a contrarian ...

"Eat your broccoli."

"Why?"

"Because I said so."

"That's not a valid reason."

Perhaps veggies aren't the best example, however; I ate so many carrots as a baby that I literally turned orange. My mom took me to a doctor, worried there was something seriously wrong. The doctor advised her that if my parents wanted to rectify the situation, they should probably lay off the carrots and attempt to get me to eat something else.

Besides this brief stint as an Oompa Loompa, I think my time as a toddler was generally decent, based on the pictures I've seen of family vacations at Disney World and me in the Little Tikes Cozy Coupe in the driveway of my childhood home. We lived on the Main Line—a perfectly manicured suburban strip of towns where wealthy Philadelphians historically escaped the heat of summer to seasonal residences, many of which now house prep schools like the one I attended from kindergarten through twelfth grade. The photos are glossy, like the idyllic settings they capture. My memories are a bit blurrier.

Remembering is hard for the best of us; sometimes it's tough to distinguish between what we actually recall versus stories we've been told, or what we've gathered from home videos. This becomes even more challenging when you add filters of drug use and trauma. While the small details and minor anecdotes remain fuzzy, though, certain major incidents that formed me stand out in my mind clear as day. But I'm getting ahead of myself...

Outside of the Kodak moments, my earliest recollections are a mixed bag. As a child I was allergic to lots of stuff, but mainly dairy products, ruling out most kid foods. Pizza and ice cream parties were always a bummer; though my mom always gave me something I could eat—even trying to make it look like the other kids' meals—I still always felt different. (I did eventually grow out of that allergy in my late teens, though, which enabled the unique experience of having boxed mac and cheese blow my mind for the first time in college.) Those allergies triggered severe asthma, requiring the occasional hospital visit and frequent use of an at-home nebulizer.

My mom named this breathing assistance machine Flounder, from the *Little Mermaid*, so I wouldn't be afraid of it. Flounder wasn't what scared me, though; it was my parents fighting all the time, and me begging my mom to leave my dad from as early as I could articulate such thoughts. My dad is prone to explosive anger, which manifests in fits of rage and tight-fisted control of everyone in his immediate vicinity. He can be goofy too, when he's not angry, and I see aspects of myself in both sides of the coin—the sense of humor and the anger, though I believe I channel mine more righteously. In any event, families aren't always as picture-perfect as they might seem.

There were definitely good times too—usually when my dad was away on business, which was frequent. I spent many sunny afternoons solving mysteries with Max and Artemis in our basement playroom, pretending to be the characters from *Scooby-*

Doo. I was always Daphne but would like to congratulate Velma for coming out as lesbian. I also loved playing Nintendo with my cousins, when we visited family, and baking with my nana. I'd help to put rainbow sprinkles on peanut butter Rice Krispies treats, my favorite, or to whip up more traditional desserts for Thanksgiving. When my hasty little hands messed up the turkey-shaped dough cut-outs for the top of a pumpkin pie, we'd eat the mistakes together. (I came out as intersex to Nana much later, finally telling her when she was ninety-nine years old. She told me that Jesus loved me no matter what, and she didn't understand why other people couldn't. I agree with her and I miss her every day.)

Nana was a whiz with a Singer sewing machine and had hand-sewn lots of custom clothes for my mom's childhood Barbies—a collection I inherited years later. One of the weirder childhood memories I have is making all my Barbies pregnant. I'd stuff the clothes I didn't like into the belly of the dresses I preferred, to give the appearance of a baby bump. I think my mom had told me from a very young age that I wouldn't be able to bear kids myself and always spoke highly of other options available, like adoption, to try to ensure that I wouldn't feel lesser for it. But even at that young age, I internalized a feeling of deficiency that some women don't assume till much later, when they struggle with fertility and find out they might not experience pregnancy themselves. Four-year-old Alicia got a big head start on all that shame and disappointment.

When I wasn't impregnating my dolls with out-of-fashion articles of clothing from their wardrobe, I was often pasting my impressive sticker collection on journals and trapper keepers made by Lisa Frank. Who *didn't* love the whole stylized, Technicolor array of animal-adorned school supplies she furnished to '90s kids? I was particularly obsessed with her cartoon dolphins and their real-life counterparts. Besides *Scooby-Doo*, *Flipper* was a favorite TV show of mine. The old 1960s series would play in the early morning hours, I believe on Nick at Nite. And I'd always be up, disrupting my poor parents' sleep, to watch it in their bed because I frequently suffered insomnia as a child. We were told that it was related to a persistent strep throat infection that I carried for quite some time; we weren't told that the early surgery to remove my reproductive organs would put me in hormone withdrawal and that hot flashes, depression, and other symptoms more common to postmenopausal women would become the norm for this kindergartener.

I'd often go to the school nurse, Mrs. Grossman, because I was crying too hard at school to stay in the classroom, or I wanted to call my mom, or I begged to be picked up early. Mom had actually started her career as a nurse but worked full time in high-powered corporate jobs to be able to afford the school tuition for me and my brother; having to duck out of meetings or leave the office midday to talk me down or take me home on a regular basis wasn't exactly good for business. As incentives to reach a certain number of days without her receiving a call, she plied me with toys, Sky Dancers in particular—little whirring fairies that actually flew and would be considered way too dangerous for generations of children born after 2000. And she'd take me most every morning to grab white powdered-sugar "bravery donuts" to give me courage to face the day (far more benign than the confidence-boosting white powder I'd turn to later in life but also far less effective).

Besides physical symptoms, I always felt different from my peers—like I never fit in anywhere—and was often reminded of it. Even in elementary school, I had a deep, raspy, some would say "sultry" voice. A lot of folks think it's hot, now that I'm older, but it was decidedly uncool back then. One afternoon my nanny Anne Brown had taken me and Max to the grocery store to pick up a whole-wheat loaf. We were rolling down the aisle to the tune of her familiar harangue, "I won't let you two eat that white bread at home; it does nothing for your health and tastes like paste," when a stranger approached her.

"Secondhand smoke kills, you know," the thirty-something mother reprimanded Anne—who looked confused but also defensive, like a lioness defending her cubs.

"Well who's smoking here?" Anne snarled in return.

The woman replied, "I heard that little girl singing as we walked in; it sounds like she blows through a pack a day."

I didn't even know what cigarettes were at that time, but I heard the point loud and clear: I was definitely different, and that difference was bad. I also remember a man once telling me I sounded like I sang in the shower—a much creepier way to call out my divergence from the norm. Then there was the time in fifth grade when two of my classmates, Josh and Andrew, told me, "You sound like a man." That one really hurt. All I ever wanted as a kid was to fit in and be just your average girl, despite knowing for as long as I could remember that I was not one.

In terms of nonstandard extracurricular activities, we visited an endocrinologist pretty much every year since my birth to monitor the progress of my development as a human. This is where my memories get much more complicated; because I wanted so badly to be normal, I suppressed a lot of the times when I felt distinctly abnormal. These memories have been tougher to access, even with the help of psychiatric support and traditional talk therapy. I also underwent a lot of experiences that folks might find disturbing, so please consider this your trigger warning and welcome to my stream of consciousness.

Intersex kids regularly visit pediatric endocrinologists over the years, ultimately inducing puberty, since—after removing our hormone-producing organs—we need outside help to reach sexual maturity. My first memory with the endo I began seeing as a preteen was when we discussed the "ideal" chest size for my frame. I was probably eleven years old, chatting with a grown man about what size breasts would look "right" in the grand scheme of my life. He kept reminding me that intersex kids with my condition, complete androgen insensitivity, always grew up to be very beautiful—often becoming models as their paid profession. (With multiple intersex friends who are or were models, I can now confirm that piece of info to be true.) He reassured me I had nothing to worry about and would undoubtedly find a great husband one day. (To be clear, I'm still searching. Again—hi, Bad Bunny.)

My next memory involves being put under anesthesia for "observation"—meaning a bunch of doctors took a peep at my genitalia for research purposes and to ascertain whether I looked "normal" enough not to require further, cosmetic surgical intervention. I have very little recollection of this "procedure," except for the pit in my stomach as I headed into the hospital for a bunch of grown strangers to look at my junk. I also remember everyone telling me after that I looked great, was very lucky, and would not need to undergo any more operations to lead a "normal" life. I would be fine just using a dilator—think a medical-grade dildo—in the comfort (shame) of my own home (closet), in order to one day be able to engage in a cis-heteronormative life involving penetrative sex. Let me tell you, this was *not* an activity most eleven- to twelve-year-olds could relate to with their pals and is something I still struggle to recollect.

My last memory from that time is being told that my endocrinologist had died but that it was okay because it was probably time for me to switch from a pediatric endocrinologist to an adult one. Since then, I've been able to find only a handful of doctors nationwide who have any experience with intersex bodies. I've had to travel back to the Northeast—at huge personal expense—to be able to access said doctors after moving elsewhere, which is something that the vast majority of Americans would never be able to afford. Plus, the doctors who *are* adequately trained in intersex anatomy don't always have our best interests in mind. They often grossly violate our bodies and our rights, in "service" to promoting some normative ideal or superior race of humans, also known as eugenics.

I've relayed all of this information pretty matter-of-factly because that's how it was always presented to me and how I first experienced all of it: sterile, medicalized, scientific, based in thinking rather than feeling. There was very little room for emotional processing, both because I wanted to pretend none of it was happening and because doctors treat us like guinea pigs in some big experiment. I do know that even if I couldn't consciously access my feelings then, they still manifest in my dreams through the same recurring nightmare I've had since childhood: people breaking into my home. I've since interpreted this to mirror the consistent violation of my most primal home, my own body, and the fact that outsiders had too much access to it during the years I needed most to feel secure. Only in recent years have I started to dig into, let alone try to understand, what all of this meant to me or how it has affected who I turned out to be.

Finding, or reclaiming, myself has often disrupted my relationships—not only with my parents but with anyone who may not want to reckon with certain things they see in the mirror. Dr. Money said our parts have the potential to "lie to their owner," like how my external appearance belies what lies within it. But our bodies are the truth. He and those who enabled him helped entrench a culture in which we need to lie about those parts rather than embrace them. That's why I never blamed my parents for what I went through, nor my individual doctors, really. I blame an oppressive society at large, one that promotes the belief that it's better to change people to fit the norm than to change the norm to accept people—that it's better to remove the traits that might lead someone to being made fun of rather than to raise kids not to make fun of those who are different.

Intersex kids who underwent surgeries aren't the only victims of soul-crushing stigma; as my friend Scout, whose body was left intact, has said: "I've been really lucky to escape the physical harm that accompanies these unnecessary surgeries, but no intersex person is free from the emotional harm that comes from living in a society that tries to cover up your existence." Parents of intersex kids are victims too, given insufficient or sometimes no tools to make these decisions that affect their kids and themselves. The choice to erase an aberration is a lot simpler than learning to navigate a world that doesn't accept–let alone accommodate–difference. Suppressing and denying someone's identity isn't the better decision, but it's a heck of a lot easier.

Denial is a shelter for some; for me, it was a prison. Generations who learned that suppression meant safety sometimes struggle to recognize that forced silence is stifling. Now fast approaching my mid-thirties, I'm guilty of not fully comprehending everything Gen Z says through their words and body movements on TikTok, but I do know that I have a lot to learn from younger generations. They're obviously our future but could also really help improve our present, if we worked harder to listen to them and understand what they have to say. Through therapy, I've realized how much of my present is stuck stunted in my past. I'm getting to know my inner child and learning how to parent her in ways that my own parents weren't necessarily equipped to. I make the same faces and poses in photos as I did back then because I am still that little girl. Part of protecting her peace now is sharing only what I think you need to know from then, no more and no less.

You might think that an intersex kid's childhood is the most important time of life to focus on, given the fact that most intersex stories are reduced to the surgery that originally mutilated us. Children are indeed innocent and in need of better protection– any protection, in the case of intersex youths in America–from violence of all forms. Even the best-intentioned of parents make decisions that might have adverse outcomes, whether it be to stay in a toxic relationship out of a desire to "keep the family together" or to alter their child's form to ensure they fit better into society's expected paradigm. But just like we tend to carry into all future relationships learned behaviors that are based on our parents' interactions, those of use who are intersex continue to face health and social inequities throughout our lives. The struggle certainly doesn't end once puberty is induced in our bodies, and the strength usually doesn't come till later. I want to include enough so that people reading this might feel less alone than I did as a child and less scared for the future. I also want to put down my pen at the end of this feeling not exploited but empowered.

If my goal was the former, I'd have shared a lot more about how my dad's treatment of my mom, and often us kids, exacerbated the misery I experienced during those years. Instead, I'll share that learning to stick up for myself and others in my household churned me out as an activist early—inculcating skills on how to fight back against injustice and oppressive systems I then had decades to hone. Intersex activists get used to sharing about our bodies and lives down to the most minute details to educate others, but we also deserve to draw a line somewhere. I don't want to write a sob story, leaving you bogged down in pity. I want to write *my* story, leaving you in awe of my power. These are *my* hands on the metaphorical steering wheel this time, and we're going to keep on cruising past the inter-sad and toward the intersexcellence. But first, let's delve into everyone's (least) favorite decade: adolescence.

TROPIC OF CAPRICORN

The Tropic of Capricorn is the southernmost latitude
on earth where the sun can be seen directly overhead;
things can go very far south, but there's still a light.

It didn't smell like teen spirit for me, when I was younger. My
lack of testosterone meant, and means, I don't produce body
odor in my pits, but the angst was fully there. Like my intersex identity, though, it may not have been immediately evident
in ways you'd traditionally expect. I didn't pierce my nose or
wear fishnets in middle school. On the weekends, I rocked Juicy
Couture tracksuits I spent all my babysitting money on to help
me fit in. For weekdays, I got green and blue rubber bands on
my braces to match the colors of our school uniform—a Black

Watch tartan pleated kilt, which I'd roll the waistband of so many times that my preteen tush would hang out. I landed in detention once when my skirt length didn't pass the "fingertip rule," but you probably wouldn't have seen much inner turmoil as an outside observer. I'll blame this on my moon sign being in Capricorn.

Apologies to any readers older than the millennial generation, as astrology is our church and y'all are about to get a quick sermon...

Astrologically, your moon sign equates with your emotional side—your feelings, intuition, and memories—and it reveals your innermost needs. Starslikeyou.com says that with the moon in Capricorn, "you are likely to have an innately serious and responsible nature... Responsibility, and all this entails, will probably form a background theme in your life. You may have had to step into a position of responsibility early in life, or received strong impressions from your parents (most usually your mother) about the need to live up to certain expectations. You may feel a deep sense of duty around supporting others." The feeling of needing to live up to expectations, and becoming an exemplary human being to do so, is an experience common not just to intersex individuals but to queer people in general. We counteract being fundamentally "flawed"—or having been taught that we are, simply by existing—by excelling in everything else that we *can* control.

This all defines my adolescence: conforming to the notions of my parents, doctors, and society as to who I should be as a young woman. I leaned into that, hard, in every way. I earned straight As in all honors classes, served as captain of varsity sports teams, held down after-school jobs to make money, and maintained leadership positions in student organizations—all in order to eventually gain the requisite acceptance into an Ivy League school. I even won the Head of the Middle School Award, which was bestowed upon the one student in our eighth-grade graduating class who demonstrated prowess and outstanding promise across all academic, athletic, and extracurricular fields. But there were cracks in the facade...

In fifth-grade health class, we had an extensive unit called "Changes," covering what puberty would look like for everyone in my class besides me. That part had been rough—learning all about how my "normal" friends' bodies would be changing, meanwhile knowing I was the odd one out. It did serve as a good primer for how I could build my fake identity as just your average female: I could start pretending I'd have a period and carry around tampons to keep up the ruse. It was tough to remember *when* to fake it, though, as we didn't have tools like calendar alerts on smartphones to serve as monthly reminders.

One afternoon in sixth grade, I went to the restroom with my then friend Stephanie during the three-minute break between math and English. At that point, girls would never pee alone; to be honest, my friends and I still rarely do in public settings. As the door swung shut to the ladies' room, Stephanie took her tube of Lip Smackers out from the breast pocket of her polo shirt. "You want some?"

"Nah," I replied. "Dr Pepper isn't my flavor. Plus I have to change my tampon before next period—Mr. Jones always makes a big deal whenever you try to leave class to use the bathroom."

I shut the door to the stall behind me, locked it, and started pulling down the Soffe shorts we all wore under our uniform kilts when I heard her say, "Wait, didn't you just have your period like two weeks ago?"

Shit. I could hear her raised eyebrow through the metal door. "Oh yeah, I don't know, I think I was just spotting then, or something? It's definitely a bloodbath in here now." *Double shit. Bloodbath?* I seriously doubted any of my friends would use that terminology to describe their time of the month.

"Weird . . ." Stephanie definitely sounded unconvinced. "You should probably go get that checked out or something."

"Totally," I managed to squeak out, as I was now hyperventilating. "I'll have my mom set up a doctor's appointment for sure." The loudspeaker announced that the next period—as in the last class before lunch, not my next fake menstruation—was starting. Literally saved by the bell.

I had lied my way out of that situation, but unfortunately that was just the beginning. As a follow-up to "Changes" in fifth grade, seventh-grade health class was dedicated to "Choices." This was my school's name for the traditional sex ed you can expect in northeastern states—thankfully not "abstinence-only," the dangerously low bar we set in the vast majority of southern schools. "Choices" involved everything from a deeper dive into reproductive anatomy to the consequences of what can happen when you use it. For this unit, we were separated into two sections by gender. While this is pretty standard, for an intersex person whose body involves organs of both sexes—and who was pretty desperately trying to avoid having to face that fact herself, let alone have any of her peers find out—just stepping foot into this divided classroom made me sweat.

There was a brief paragraph in our textbook that referenced "sexual anomalies," but it mentioned only Klinefelter syndrome as an example, not my own intersex variation of CAIS. *Phew*. The last thing I wanted was to acknowledge my own reality in a reading, let alone see my peers' reaction to it. The day our homework covered this chapter also included the classic condom-on-the-banana demonstration in class. At least with everyone laughing uncomfortably, no one would notice the beads of perspiration forming on my brow, right? I forced a hollow chuckle when Abigail cracked inappropriate jokes from across the room, a welcome distraction that took any attention away from my desk in the back left corner.

Mrs. Marino, visibly exhausted, attempted to regain control of the students. "Okay, ladies, I know you think this is all fun and games. But using a condom is the best way, besides total abstinence, to ensure that none of you ends up pregnant anytime soon." She continued, a little more forcefully above the persistent giggling, "Next class I'll show you what that would entail when we watch the *Miracle of Life* video. I think after seeing what it's like to give birth, you girls will wish you took this condom conversation a bit more seriously!"

The fits of laughter evolved into a collective groan, as some of the barely teenagers processed what they were in for in next week's "Choices." "I can't believe we need to watch this!" Olivia whispered to me with a look of disdain. "Our dads don't even have to when it happens in real life." "Totally," I choked out through the panic that had started to grip my throat. I knew I'd never be giving birth one day and truly had no desire to watch what I'd be missing out on, certainly not in front of my classmates. *But does everyone agree with Olivia? Or should I act like this is cool—like I'm cool with it—for the sake of keeping up appearances? How would a "normal" girl act in this situation?* *Beep.* Saved by the bell, again.

I now had seven full days to agonize over the appropriate way to handle this situation. Sleepless nights only fueled the anxiety that kept building in my chest. I avoided seeing friends over the weekend, feigning a cold, to dodge any potential discussion of the class to come. But Tuesday came, and as I walked into the third-floor science classroom, I started to feel lightheaded. "All right, everyone. We are going to start the video, and I ask you to keep your reactions to yourself," Mrs. Marino welcomed the class; her disbelief in the prospect of that actually happening was palpable. "If I hear laughing, screaming, or any inappropriate reactions, I'll ask you to leave and you'll receive a demerit—anything too disruptive and I'll make it a detention."

Phew, okay. She's expecting folks to take this badly. That means their eyes will be on the screen and not on me. As she clicked "play," my sweats started again, and what had begun as light-headed was verging on dizzy. I rested my head on the desk.

"Alicia, are you okay?" I looked up and my eyes met Mrs. Marino's. Nearly everyone else was turning in my direction too.

Shit. Think of something... but the room was starting to get hazy.

"I had a cold this weekend and I think I'm not better yet," I mustered in the teacher's general direction, through blurred vision. "I, I think I should probably head to the nurse actually."

"Okay, do you need someone to go with you?" Mrs. Marino asked, noticeably concerned.

"No, no, of course not. I'll be back in a few."

I started to rise, awkwardly, with both hands gripping the desk for balance. *The quicker I get out of here, the quicker they'll turn back to the video and forget I even left.* My mind was racing but my feet felt like lead weights as I stumbled out of the classroom. *Just make it to the stairwell—can't be more than a few yards.* My vision started fading. *Maybe the elevator is a better bet.* But the darkness was expanding too fast. *Okay, let's just sit down in the hallway and wait for this to pass.* I leaned against the wall and slumped to the floor.

"Alicia? Alicia!" Emma was standing above me. Her lips were pursed tight but her eyes were wide with fear.

"Yeah, yeah, I'm fine."

How is it possible to feel so cold and clammy at the same time? I tried to lift my head. *So heavy.*

"You don't look fine," Emma said. "I'm going to get someone else out here so we can help get you to the nurse."

"No, no, no!" I frantically sought to reassure her. *You can't let more people find out you literally fainted during* The Miracle of Life! "If you can just give me a hand and help me up, I'll head down in the elevator—all good here!"

She grabbed my hand and pulled my dead weight into a limp standing position. "Here, take my arm and at least let me walk you down there."

I was truly grateful that it was Emma who found me. *Imagine if it had been Abigail or someone who gossips.* "Thanks, Em."

She pressed the button to call the elevator but I heard footsteps behind me. *Oh no, Joe and Neal!* As two of the most notorious class clowns approached us, I could see them registering that I was leaning on Emma's shoulder, about a head shorter than my own.

"What's going on with you?" Neal asked, locking eyes with Joe. I could see their wheels starting to spin.

"I'm taking her to the nurse," Emma replied. "She just passed out in the hallway! Thankfully it was during the *Miracle of Life* video—I needed an excuse to get out of there." In a well-meaning attempt to make me feel better about being accompanied to the first floor, she had just opened the floodgates.

"Alicia fainted during *The Miracle of Life*? No way!" Neal was grinning ear to ear. "That's too good!"

As he and Joe both turned to run down the stairs, off to whatever mischief had brought them out of class in the middle of third period, they looked back at me. *Why can't I just disappear, right here—right now?* I knew that this horrific situation would not end here. Lunch was in an hour, and half of my grade would know by then. "I had a cold this weekend and I think I'm still feeling it," I called after them. But the damage was done. By the afternoon, the girl who wanted nothing more than to fly under the radar would become known as the girl who couldn't handle watching life's most miraculous process that she would never experience.

I guess I can tell people Dad almost fainted watching me be born? Having them think I get woozy at the sight of blood was better than anything connecting me to uneasiness about giving birth. Any conversations like that would risk crumbling the careful facade I'd constructed and struggled to maintain for years.

The nurse could diagnose no illness, given that I *had* no illness. Only in hindsight have I realized that I suffered a panic attack, triggered by the fear of being found out. She excused me from the rest of science class, thank God, and ordered that I rest and hydrate till lunch. Once I'd downed sufficient Dixie cups of water to satisfy her and my color returned to normal, she pushed me out of her office and in the direction of the cafeteria. "You should get some food in your stomach. I'll watch you walk over; if you get dizzy again, just give me a wave." I had planned to spend lunch period hiding in the locker room, dreading the wolves. Now there was no escaping my fate...

I slunk into the dining hall, avoiding eye contact with anyone at the table of guys I heard snickering in my direction. Josh got up from his plate of pasta to cut me off as I beelined toward the stack of lunch trays.

"Hey Alicia, we heard you fainted during *The Miracle of Life*?!"

I couldn't even catch the rest of what followed through the cloud of laughter. My face turned as red as his spaghetti sauce, and I immediately turned on my heel to skip the hot food line, sprinting straight to the salad bar. I tossed a few leaves of lettuce onto my plate, adding a sprinkling of shaved carrots (old habits die hard) and a pool of Italian dressing. I then tripped and almost dumped my paltry meal all over Natalie and Katie, as I attempted to find a seat at my usual table without averting my gaze from the floor. Thankfully, a few of the girls reassured me that they couldn't imagine ever wanting to put their bodies through what they'd seen in the video, and the conversation veered elsewhere. The collective attention span of the seventh grade had fizzled, and my nerves followed suit. By the next day, there was someone new to ridicule, and my anxiety returned to everyday levels.

Speaking of ridicule, if you've ever seen *Mean Girls*, my school had our own equivalent of the Plastics—just a few years younger and more than three times as many of them: the Foxy 14. Though we weren't quite as vindictive, I'm embarrassed to relay I was a member and probably still have my branded sweatpants somewhere in storage as evidence. Given that there were fourteen of us, the hierarchy was a bit more complicated than in the movie, but our Regina George equivalent was the aforementioned Abigail Poole.

Middle school is already tough, but it's even tougher when you're trying to keep up with the wardrobe of a dozen other girls whose parents own all Philly's major league teams while your own are hustling to meet tuition checks. But Abigail made my life hell to the point where I tried, unsuccessfully, to transfer to a different school. I could relay numerous stories about how she tortured me—including the time she squirted a huge glob of white Blistex lip balm on my face in history class and immediately called out to the teacher, "Mr. Schultz, I just saw Alicia come back from the bathroom with Ryan Anderson." In case your mind's not as evil as hers: she was insinuating I'd just given a blow job to my fellow classmate in the restroom, when I hadn't even had my first *kiss* yet.

The Foxy 14 remained more or less intact for years, besides a few substitutions, as we lost some members to other high schools and gained new students to our class in ninth grade. We rolled deep and stuck together pretty exclusively–bonded by fear and friendship, depending on the day. Most of us kept up pristine appearances at school but would also nick our parents' liquor to spike the caramel Frappuccinos we drank while strolling the King of Prussia Mall after class. Many of us were teachers' pets on campus but also made out with older boys at parties, once we left school premises (or sometimes strategically tucked away in vacant classrooms).

At one group sleepover around this time, we all drank a good amount of some disgusting lethal mixture of whatever booze our parents never touched and I got wasted enough to admit to two of my friends that I was infertile. I believe I told them that I'd fought childhood cancer, which led to the removal of my reproductive organs–a pretty intense lie that evolved from doctors having told my parents my testes might become cancerous someday. As I understand it, this is a pretty common ruse among the intersex community. I never explained that I had XY chromosomes, though, or that I was born with balls; I couldn't admit that to myself yet, let alone to anyone else. My friends were actually really supportive, if I remember correctly (I was pretty blacked out), and promised not to tell anyone else–which I don't think they ever did. But this lie was emblematic of how much shame and stigma I felt, simply for being alive, and how these forces drove me into some toxic behaviors that would continue for many years.

I blame the WASP culture I was born into, which promotes suppressing any and all divergence from normality and masking any unpleasant feelings with copious amounts of alcohol. Beyond my own discrepancy from the norm in terms of sex, my brother—who uses both "he" and "they" pronouns—was always pretty out there. As a musician, he often had blue hair or sometimes wore stuff that didn't make much sense to me but aligned with a vibe he was trying to give off. One time I remember he tried to shave his legs in middle school, and my dad threw him out of the bathtub, pinned him against the wall, and screamed so loud about how unacceptable it was that Max would certainly never attempt it again.

These rage blackouts were not uncommon in our house, especially in the wake of my mom, brother, or me doing something deemed "imperfect." For example, my dad would come into my closet unannounced and throw all the clothing out of my drawers and onto the floor saying it was folded improperly; or if my mom put something in the "wrong" cupboard, it would elicit a screaming match that would have my brother up in his room wearing his noise-canceling headphones and me crying myself to sleep. But the particular instance of my brother trying to express himself and his gender through alternate grooming practices—and having this met with violence—is pretty illustrative of how my own perceived imperfection was effectively stamped out too. Denial was, and remains, a very strong coping skill that my parents exercised in the wake of any issue. My mom has supplemented this denial with drinking at times, so I guess I come by this habit honestly.

Besides the experimentation with alcohol that began in my tween years, by high school I'd found other ways to act out. During my freshman year, I "dated" Jeremy—a senior known as one of the biggest partiers in his grade. He drove a Jeep with no doors and blasted music out of it at full volume as we rolled around town smoking joints or en route to parties in the off-campus apartments of Villanova University students nearby. My parents were extremely strict and did everything in their power to try to prevent me from getting into dangerous situations, not counting the violence at home. But, as it turns out, having to conceal your identity makes you really good at covering other things up too.

At school, I effectively masked my inner turmoil, partially by funneling my proclivity for hiding my true self into a more socially acceptable skill: acting. I had played parts in various middle school musicals, including a junior leading role as Mabel in *The Pajama Game*, but persistent vocal nodules had ultimately thwarted my future performance as an alto. I was lucky to find a powerful alternative a year after my last singing role. With three years of Latin under my belt by the time I hit freshman year (shout-outs to Mrs. Smith and the late, great Dr. Iozzo—two of the best teachers I've had), I joined Ms. Miller's class on the ancient language. Ms. Miller happens to be the now famous author Madeline Miller, whose bestselling modern interpretations of the classics from *Circe* to *The Song of Achilles* challenge everything from misogyny to heteronormativity. The way she taught ninth-grade Latin was imbued with the same values, and all the queer kids in school—out or not—flocked to her classroom after school for Shakespeare rehearsal.

A master of old languages from all eras and locations—from Greek to Old English—Ms. Miller had a passion for helping us find universal themes within old texts in a way that made each of us feel less alone. She helped me find a penchant for the written word through translating the epic poem *The Aeneid* and for the spoken word through interpreting Shakespeare's works in front of an audience. I wasn't able to process my own emotions yet, but I felt Portia's pain deeply as I stabbed myself onstage in *Julius Caesar*; I hadn't accessed pride and strength in my own life yet but was able to try those feelings on as Volumnia in *Coriolanus*. The love of Shakespeare's work she instilled in me would continue through college, where I played Maria in *Love's Labour's Lost* alongside other students and professional Equity actors. It also helped me cultivate public speaking skills I still use to this day when testifying at the legislature or delivering remarks at conferences and rallies. The love of Latin she helped me crystalize paid even more lasting dividends.

I'd been placed in her standard-level Latin class, as opposed to honors, on the basis of a lack of self-confidence I'd developed in predominately male classrooms throughout middle school. By high school, even more young women had dropped the language; I was one of only five who continued as Latin scholars after ninth grade. Ms. Miller helped me find my voice and learn to trust it, shepherding me into Mr. Rich's subsequent honors Latin classes for the remaining three years of high school. Mr. Rich, also a staunch feminist and wonderful mentor, took me and my friend Meghan under his wing and helped us reach the top of the class—neck and neck with the two male students who'd land the valedictorian and salutatorian spots at graduation. Not only did I gain rhetorical skills from the great Cicero that I still use when I lobby against Republican lawmakers, but I learned how to succeed in male-dominated systems, perhaps the most useful aptitude I gleaned from those years.

Outside of school was a whole 'nother scenario. The Alicia who shined in the classroom versus the Alicia who showed up at parties couldn't have appeared more different. My acting skills served me well in leading my double life. I became an expert at sneaking around and mostly got away with it—except for a party or two when my mom received a call from my rightfully concerned friends and had to pick me up and revive me from alcohol poisoning. Eventually, I started to develop a reputation among not just the student body, but their families as well. Word eventually made its way to the school's administration, and I was mandated weekly visits with the guidance counselor, to help turn me off the "bad path" I'd stumbled onto.

The instincts of the adults in my life—that I was on a slippery slope and was jeopardizing all the "perfection" I'd cultivated with hard partying ways—weren't wrong. The thing is, no school therapist would have been able to help me unearth the source of my pain and reason for acting out, when my parents and medical doctors were all enlisted in helping to cover it up. When you're gay, or trans, chances are the elders in your life might not figure it out until you're ready to come clean with that info. When you're intersex, everyone in positions of power tasked with keeping you safe and healthy—within your own family and the medical industry—knows about your "defect" early on, often from the second you enter this world. Regardless of their intentions, the people who shape you know about the closet you're in from Day 1 and shove you deeper and deeper into it. How could these people save me from myself when they were the ones preventing me from figuring out who that self really was?

Beyond all the drinking to drown dark thoughts, I also obliterated them through the early adoption of a stoner persona. Not a pothead, because I kept my shit together, but a stoner; this linguistic distinction meant something to me at the time. Not only did I hit bowls frequently with my older "boyfriend," I also started rolling and toking blunts with a group of guy friends I started palling around with—one of whom would later become my first love. We'd roll around in our parents' cars, listening to Lil Wayne and even mimicking his own vehicles for consumption through the construction of "purple blunts": weed-packed dutches dipped in promethazine cough syrup. These dangerous concoctions often knocked us into a stupor after just one hit—just the ticket for someone trying desperately to escape her inner demons.

In hindsight, I marvel at the fact that no one got hurt—though I did lose one good friend to opioid addiction years later—and that we avoided any run-ins with the cops during these shenanigans. I now credit this to residing in wealthier, primarily white suburbs, less subject to overpolicing. I can't imagine how the Black students at my school felt, witnessing the appropriation of some of the wildest behaviors of one of their cultural icons and knowing that they couldn't safely follow suit with the reckless abandon we exhibited. The majority of my significant interactions with people of color in that era were with my co-workers at Bertucci's Italian restaurant—with whom I frequently partied and to whom I even sold weed once in a while when they were out.

The fear of punishment at school and significant white privilege kept me out of enough trouble to avoid ending up on that "bad path" the guidance counselor warned of. Had I been born into less financial comfort—or attended a school less dedicated to ensuring students didn't fall through the cracks—things could have gone very differently. I perhaps could have spun out to the point of ending up unhoused, as is the desperate reality of so many young folks in our community (research shows that LGBTQIA+ youth have a 120 percent higher risk of experiencing some form of homelessness). I work so hard on ending homelessness today through my role on Austin's Human Rights Commission because I realize how close I was, how close we all are, to landing in a similar situation; what keeps each of us housed is not some moral superiority or exemplary work ethic, it is privilege.

Fear of God—or of my parents and our school's headmaster—kept me on a path that was relatively straight, if not narrow. It didn't keep me actually happy, though, nor was it necessarily the right path for *me*. The rest of my adolescence and early adulthood not only was lived under the influence of heavy drug and alcohol use, but was defined by the desires of who everyone else wanted me to be. I went to Cornell University because it was the "best school" I got into. But between heavy academic pressure and the fact that it snowed in Ithaca from October often till after my birthday in May, I wasn't super happy there. Although heavy drinking in college is normalized, I think anyone who knew me during those years would say I definitely took it to another level.

Besides substance abuse, I also engaged in reckless sexual practices. I didn't have the fear of pregnancy, so I wasn't always great about condom use. This was risky not only to my physical health but to my mental health too. The years from when I first became sexually active at age fourteen, way younger than I should have, to when I came out more than a decade later weren't characterized by how a young woman deserved to experience pleasure. After I "lost my virginity"—a total construct, but a very real rite of passage at the time—all the senior girls wouldn't leave me alone, especially because the person was three years older than me. For the rest of freshman year, I walked the halls with a target on my back and suffered relentless "slut-shaming" for the first time. The experience damaged my self-esteem, making me more vulnerable to taunts and leading me to believe that I was, in fact, a slut. I proceeded to act accordingly for the rest of my teen years and most of my early twenties.

In hindsight I see that I wasn't promiscuous because I was a self-affirmed heaux, exercising my God-given right to pleasure (power to these women, fighting the double-standard of sexual activity for our gender!), but because my sexual experiences were based on the need for validation from others. Yes, as a thin, blond white woman I have always been conventionally attractive in the way that Western society defines it. But in those early years, I used sex to authenticate that I *was*, in fact, a woman— measured by how desirable I was to the male gaze. Society also equates womanhood with certain rigid factors, more related to one's assigned sex at birth than to gender. For me, knowing that regardless of what I looked like on the outside, I had XY chromosomes in my cells and no womb in my belly threatened my validity as a viable sexual or romantic partner. Unlearning the idea that I'm inherently unlovable is something I'm still working on to this day.

I didn't have the tools yet to learn to love myself. Around this time, though, I started on my journey of helping other broken beings. Since I wasn't quite able to accept grace and compassion, it felt easier to funnel these feelings toward abandoned animals. It all started when I fell for that ASPCA commercial with Sarah McLachlan—you know the one, with all the one-eyed dogs limping in cages, accented by Sarah's devastating crooning and culminating in a 1-800 number to call. I was seventeen the year it aired and had worked a few years at minimum wage since reaching the legal age to work in Pennsylvania—babysitting and working at a French bakery, before the Italian restaurant—so I had a few (key word: few) dollars to my name. I dialed the help line and gave them my debit card number to authorize a recurring monthly donation that far exceeded my ability to give. Very soon after, I faced for the first time the harsh reality that exploits low-income individuals and apparently fledgling animal-care philanthropists: overdraft fees.

Since channeling my altruism through charitable contributions hadn't worked out so well, I decided to take a different approach. That summer, I went to Greece with my neighbor Artemis, her brother, and her parents—basically my adopted second family—as a graduation gift from my own parents. The country is stunning and overrun with stray cats. Soon after arriving in Kalamata, I stumbled upon a tiny—filthy—kitten in a gutter on the side of the road, so small it hadn't even opened its eyes yet. *What a sweet little baby.* I scooped it up with no concern for bugs or disease and carried it with me in one hand straight back to the house of Artemis's γιαγιά. I didn't exactly have a plan yet, but I was sure her grandma could help me make one.

As it turns out, γιαγιά's plans didn't involve welcoming a potentially pestilence-ridden pet into her home. After some initial shrieking and shoving me and my new baby outside, she gave me an old birdcage to house the kitty and told me I could keep it outdoors under certain conditions: first and foremost, I had to wash it immediately; then, I'd have to take the kitten at the earliest possible availability to have it examined for illness. I easily agreed and proceeded to give the itty-bitty angel a sponge bath, only to discover it was actually orange and striped—not, in fact, dusty street-gutter brown. I then learned from Artemis's mom, Athina, that there were multiple veterinarians in the family—Greeks have a cousin for everything—and we could take my little one in to be seen the following morning.

The veterinary appointment was confusing, given that the only Greek I'd learned at that point was how to express that I was hungry, full, or certain other key phrases all related to food. I did keep hearing the same word over and over, though, in the conversation between Athina and the doctor—one that sounded suspiciously like "Chlamydia." "Athina, what does Chlamydia mean in Greek?" I asked, earnestly believing it perhaps meant "cat" or some other relevant term.

"Chlamydia means Chlamydia," she replied. "The cat has Chlamydia, Alicia."

Oy. It turns out the kitty had contracted the infection from its mother at birth and had it all over its eyes, which I'd gently yet meticulously scrubbed clean the day before. Maybe γιαγιά had had a point after all.

Luckily, the feline STI was pretty easily curable, so the vet wrote a prescription and asked whether we knew which shelter we'd be surrendering him to. "Shelter?!" I exclaimed, upon hearing Athina's translation. "There's no way we're giving this baby away!" Γιαγιά already had too many animals at home so I asked about the process of taking him back stateside—determined to find a better way even knowing full well that my dad was deathly allergic to cats and there was no way he'd accept a foreign animal into our home. Our vet cousin outlined the process of applying for a kitty passport, including the necessary quarantine he'd have to undergo before being able to cross any national borders. We took the little guy back to γιαγιά's home, and I ultimately persuaded Athina and her husband, Antonis, to take him to their own home in the US by the end of my stay.

I named the cat Spakolopsis. I thought this was how you said "please" in Greek (it's actually *se parakalo*)—as in, "Please, adopt this cat for me and take him with you across an ocean to your house, since I can't bear to let him go." Though my pleading was ultimately successful, the name needed help—the butchered Greek sounded more like a dinosaur than a kitten and didn't exactly roll off the tongue. Artemis's younger brother, Takis, had the idea to shorten my proposed name to Spaki, which stuck. Spaki currently lives in Princeton, New Jersey, fat and happy, with no memory of his early days in the street—let alone of his original savior.

Since then, I've rescued stray dogs in countries throughout the Americas and brought one into my own home for good: my infamous nine-pound shadow, Chiquita. I attribute this insatiable desire to assist lost souls with finding their way home to providing the sort of help I wish I had received at the time, the first step on my path to healing; I wouldn't find a real home in my own body till many years later. I also blame Bob Barker—the original host of one of my favorite TV shows growing up—who'd end each episode of *The Price Is Right* with the familiar refrain, "Help control the animal population! Have your pet spayed or neutered."

I was scarred early by my own sterilization surgery, not just physically but mentally. As I worked to heal the emotional wounds decades afterward, I also wanted to heal the original source of all this pain. In order to reclaim the scar, I decided to tattoo over it—kind of like knocking down a monument dedicated to an oppressive figure and erecting the statue of a liberator in its place. I finally found my freedom living in and traveling through countries that all happen to be cut by the Tropic of Capricorn, the latitude of my moon sign. As I trekked through Chile, Brazil, South Africa, and Mozambique, some of my happiest memories include driving past road signs that read "You are now crossing the Tropic of Capricorn" in various languages. Thousands of miles from "home," I felt the most me. It felt right to superimpose that feeling over the site of where I was first robbed of a part of myself.

I had the area tattooed while I was in Chicago for my first ever intersex rally, decades after the surgery that attempted to erase that part of my identity. Lost as I was in my youth, I did ultimately find myself in adulthood, even if it took many years and many miles to do so. I think a lot of queer folks have to distance themselves from where they were born in order to own who they were born to be. I showed the tattoo artist the scar from my castration, running across my lower abdomen where he might expect to find a womb. He drew a circle with a line running through it—aligning the mark of where they'd stitched me to the point on the circle where the Tropic of Capricorn transverses Earth. The Tropic of Capricorn is the southernmost latitude where the sun can be seen directly overhead, symbolizing what I wish I'd known in those toughest years: things can go very far south, but there's still a light.

FIGA

The figa—originally a representation of female (or intersex) genitalia—is meant to distract the devil so he won't steal the wearer's soul. A mark of protection; a symbol of resistance.

The *figa de guiné* is a symbol often worn as an amulet for protection in the state of Bahia, where I lived in northeast Brazil during my semester abroad in college—a pivotal period in my transition from childhood naivete into the harsh reality of womanhood. One internet site (www.jewelryfashiontips.com) describes the figa as "a closed fist, with the thumb going through the index and middle fingers. It is a representation of a woman's genitalia and sex. . . . It is said to ward off the 'evil eye' and bring protection to the wearer. Basically, the gesture is supposed to be so offensive that it scares off the 'evil.' Interestingly, Brazil and Portugal also see this amulet as a good luck symbol." Another site (lucky-charms.org) writes that "the obscene gesture depicted in the Figa symbol is believed to distract the devil so he won't steal the wearer's soul." While these descriptions that I grabbed off the internet—and the origin story of the figa symbol itself—are problematic in quite a few ways (women can have any sort of genitalia, for instance), this particular interpretation is interesting to me. The figa is also visually similar to the raised fist that, in the United States, symbolizes resistance and unites communities rebelling against oppressive forces seeking to steal their souls.

My rebellious streak may have begun in high school, but I was still a rebel without a cause. It's not that my acting out didn't generate from a valid place, my pain and loneliness, but I didn't yet have a cause to throw it at. Although I was an officer in a few student groups, including STAND (Students Taking Action Now: Darfur)—a student- and youth-led movement to end mass atrocities like the genocide in Darfur, Sudan—most of how I spent my time was an effort to make myself a more attractive candidate for college acceptance. That, and partying. I was still almost a decade out from becoming an activist in earnest—from truly caring about the plight of a community I hadn't yet assumed as my own and of others who face oppression. For now, I'd settle for sneaking out from my basement or from houses of friends with less strict parents to drink myself into oblivion and still somehow make it to crew practice before school the next morning.

I placed well in enough rowing regattas and had sufficient extracurricular activities fluffing my resume to make it into a handful of great colleges, ultimately deciding on Cornell. I really wanted to go to Rice University in Houston, but my parents thought an Ivy League degree would serve me better in the long run and they wanted me closer to home; I guess I wasn't meant to make it to Texas for a few more years.

Cornell is probably a great school for some people. The campus is situated in New York's Finger Lakes region, a stunningly beautiful part of the country, nestled between cavernous gorges. Upstate New York, however, is known for its long winters. Students go home for the summer, by far the best time of year to be in Ithaca, and are present during the harshest weather. I've realized since that I suffer from a kind of depression called seasonal affective disorder (SAD). Austin's more mild winters (save the occasional winter storm that leaves us without power or water, brutally unprotected by failing infrastructure our state government continually fails to fix ...) are way more my vibe.

Speaking of warmer climates, during the first week of orientation at Cornell, I met a group of Brazilians who became my first and longest standing guy friends at school. Between the frustration of not being able to understand their language when they'd shoot the shit playing video games and my understanding that studying abroad in their country would entail swapping a daily trek through the snow to get to class with a stroll down the beach to do so, I decided to start learning Portuguese. My original reason for choosing to attend Cornell was heavily influenced by their top-three linguistics program and the fact that linguists were in high demand for foreign service–oriented careers. I thought I might want to join the Central Intelligence Agency, based on my high school acting chops and ability to learn languages on the fly. I spoke pretty fluent Spanish at that point, my high school classes supplemented by working in restaurants after school and learning how to charm the line cooks into making me free food during my shift. Plus, I figured that disguising myself my whole life would likely make me a pretty great spy.

I eventually took enough history classes to realize that the CIA had played a role in propping up dictatorships around the world and might not actually be a good fit for someone who had a real issue with following rules. But I stuck with my linguistics major for the first half of my tenure at Cornell, which often involved squawking alone in my dorm room—learning how properly to pronounce all of the International Phonetic Alphabet (basically a categorization of every sound that exists in every known language in the world, better known as those strange characters you see at the beginning of a Wikipedia definition). When I wasn't creeping out my roommates by repeatedly clicking at myself in the mirror, I could be found at my job with the Cornell Annual Fund asking alumni for money or running through the wilderness on and surrounding campus.

I ran cross-country in high school to maintain conditioning for my primary sport, crew, during the off-season. But it was really my mornings and evenings traversing thousands of acres of backcountry in the Cornell Botanic Gardens when I discovered my true love of running. On one occasion, I bumped into fellow Cornell alum Bill Nye deep in the woods and jogged alongside him for the greater portion of an hour, as he pointed out his favorite flowers, trees, and other Science Guy stuff (thanks too,

Bill, for exploring the spectrum of sex in your recent Netflix special!). Usually, though—unlike team training in high school—I took to the trails solo.

Most days I'd run in the range of ten miles through the forests and fields—fueled by the ungodly amounts of Adderall I consumed to maintain my rigorous school and partying schedule—to the point where I looked thinner than what most would consider healthy and was probably taxing my body more than was safe. I was literally running myself to the bone but was truly happiest with my feet treading the dirt. When I used to strap on my shoes and sprint out of the house to escape my parents fighting, my mom would call it "running from my problems." Living on my own during college, I learned to not just run away from the bad, but to run toward something positive.

When I often struggled to keep up my grades in Advanced Microeconomics for Engineers or Policy Analysis and Management Statistics, or to remember where I'd left my parka (or my wallet, or my underwear) after a night bouncing from frat basement to frat basement, running gave me a sense of control. It gave me time and space for myself in a world where—between navigating roommates' shower schedules and crowded libraries and fake-ID-riddled bars—I often struggled to find them. Training my body to a point where I could run up any hill and heading deep into the forest where I could turn any which way I pleased, I gained a sense of power and freedom. Being out in nature was healing, and in this one area of my life, I wasn't competing against everyone else, as I had during high school races; I was running just for me.

Trail running became my solace during an otherwise bleak era of my life. By the time junior year hit, I had designed my own major (the only student my year in the College of Arts and Sciences granted permission to do so) focused on political economy in Latin America. I'd also mastered my Portuguese well enough to spend a semester in Brazil. I was ecstatic when I boarded the plane to São Paulo, where I would complete a monthlong language intensive to prepare for six months of classes alongside Brazilian students in Bahia. When I exited the ten-hour flight from New York City, not even the fact that my luggage was lost could put a damper on my excitement to have finally arrived. As I attempted to navigate the baggage claims office with what was still pretty broken Portuguese, a kindly Paulista—someone from Brazil's largest city, São Paulo—stepped in to help.

"What brings you to Brazil?" Antônio, a forty-something in jeans and a polo, asked me—in English, thank God.

"I'm here for an exchange program for a semester! Eventually I'll head to Bahia after about a month in São Paulo. What were you doing in New York?"

"I was there for a conference representing my marketing agency," Antônio replied; I saw an opportunity.

"I hate to ask for more help when you've already been *muito gentil* in helping me recover my bags, but I'm always looking for opportunities to work on top of school to help with my bills, and the opportunity to *me estagiar* in a Brazilian company would be huge. Does your agency offer internships?"

"Given how good your Portuguese is"—it truly wasn't at that point; this is something all Brazilians say to anyone who has gotten down at least a couple of key phrases in their language, probably because so few Americans endeavor to learn it—"I think we could consider something. Here's my card; send me an email, *por gentileza*."

I share this interaction not only to show how I was lucky enough to land an internship with a credible brand management group within five minutes of landing in-country but also to show the nature of Brazilian hospitality. As someone raised in the US Northeast—where random kindness from a stranger is viewed as suspect—I found the effusive friendliness demonstrated by the people of my new country of residence disarming. This charm is a natural quality of most every Brazilian I've met and is a beautiful thing; but I also let it lull me—a twenty-year-old woman who'd grown up in a crime-free suburb and then attended an equally cloistered university but would now be living in a foreign country for the first time—into a false sense of security.

This immediate sense of safety gained strength upon meeting my first host family, a mother and her daughter, who happened to be my age. My host mom, Olívia, was a sweet and gregarious woman who was excited to make me stroganoff (a Brazilian take on the original Russian stew, this one made with chicken and traditionally topped—perhaps strangely to foreigners, but deliciously—with fried potato sticks, equivalent to crushed Lay's). My host sister, Laís, tutored her peers in English and was addicted to American pop culture. Besides showing me the necessary bus routes to reach my new internship and classes every day, they helped me with my homework and introduced me to classic Brazilian cultural experiences every night. When

Laís invited me to visit Santos, a nearby beach city, to spend the weekend with a guy she'd been seeing and his family, I didn't think twice.

This next part I won't delve into in great detail, both because I've mentally blocked a lot of it out and because I don't owe anyone trauma porn. I also imagine many folks reading this may also be survivors of sexual assault, given that one in five American women—not counting additional folks of all genders—are raped while in college. All I'll say is that one night in Santos, while out with Laís, her boy toy, and his friends, I fell unconscious, only to awaken in a drugged haze on the beach with two of them on top of me. I managed to push them off me and somehow stumble back to the home where we were staying. Before even registering concern for my own safety, my first thought was what I would tell my boyfriend, Mike.

Mike and I had dated since the end of high school, long-distance while he attended Penn State, and even longer distance while I studied abroad in Brazil and he spent a semester in Barcelona. He was already upset with me for choosing to go to South America, since I also speak Spanish and could have joined him in Europe—giving us six months together rather than adding an ocean of distance to the physical space already separating us. Immediately following that trauma on the beach, my anxiety spiked as I sat ruminating what to do. My internal panic broke when Laís came out of the bedroom—until I saw her face. She paused only long enough to tell me how disappointed she was in me for ditching her earlier that evening—considering all she and her family had done for me—before she headed to the shower.

She left me in the foyer, still wearing the clothes I'd hastily pulled back on after fleeing the two men who'd violated me. I had never felt so alone.

After an icy car ride back to São Paulo the next morning—me lost in my own thoughts and Laís refusing to talk to me anyway—we arrived back at her home. The coping chemicals that had flooded my body started to dissipate, and I registered the pain in my genitals for the first time. I rushed to the bathroom and found blood in my swimsuit bottoms and sores on my labia. My first instinct was to text one of our exchange program wranglers, Ana, who was openly queer, had tattoos and piercings, and felt the least judgmental of anyone I knew in the near vicinity. I told her I had had unprotected sex, was worried about contracting a sexually transmitted infection, and wanted to seek testing immediately. She jumped into help mode, assisting me with setting up an appointment with a doctor and even offering to accompany me. I'm so grateful for her being there at one of the lowest points of my life. It turns out that although I remained STI free, my labia were severely torn as one of the men who'd assaulted me had braces.

When I tried to tell Mike what had happened, he blamed me for my carelessness. I honestly have no idea how I framed the experience for him, as I hadn't even been able to process it yet myself. In fact, I'm still working on it. An added layer of complexity to an already terrible situation is that many times throughout my childhood grown men had invaded my personal space; I stripped for doctors as a kid so they could poke and prod my most intimate parts. This meant that I was already more used to violation of my body's boundaries than most people; I was almost numb to it and adept at finding ways to obscure such invasion and trauma from other people because I'd already hidden such experiences with doctors from the rest of the world for most of my life.

Considering all of this, I don't think I registered what happened to me as rape, at the time; I am certain I didn't relay it to Mike in such stark yet fitting terms. But between his response, which was to ask for space to consider whether or not he'd break up with me, and Laís's, I started to blame myself. *I was drinking that night… I got myself into this situation. Now I'm gonna have to get myself out of it.* Telling my parents definitely wasn't an option; they'd just try to get me to come back from Brazil. I'd be leaving São Paulo in just a few days to start the semester in Salvador. Bahia was three states away—half the length of the United States in distance from that beach. I couldn't let this trip be a failure, and this was a chance at a fresh start. *I just won't drink once I get there and for the rest of my time here; I'll tell Mike that too and maybe he'll trust me enough to stay with me after all. Everything will be fine. I'll be fine.*

I definitely wasn't fine, but at least I had a plan to distract me from my pain. All the other students in my exchange program thought it was weird that I stopped drinking right before we took off for the party capital of Brazil—of the world, really, as Salvador hosts the largest annual Carnaval street party on the planet. But as soon as I dropped my bags into my new room, I broke out my computer and researched local Alcoholics Anonymous programs—finding one regularly hosted at a church nearby.

I ended up attending weekly—always hiding from friends and

members of my new host family where I was headed, attempting to keep up in a language I was still learning to grasp and claiming an alcoholic identity I wasn't even sure fit my circumstances. But taking some sort of logical action felt like something in my power to help atone for all the feelings that inevitably hit me every night as I lay down to sleep. *I just need Mike to forgive me. And I can forget about Laís and Olívia since I'll never see them again. I'll just keep getting STI tests, to make sure I stay negative, and never drink again, to avoid ever being back in that position. Everything will be fine. I'll be fine.*

This was long before the heyday of the #MeToo movement, and I had zero context for how to navigate what had happened to me. I had no support and was, in retrospect, doing nothing to actually heal. I was simply ticking boxes on ways to mitigate the fallout of my rape, in order to keep the self-loathing at bay. One of the ways I numbed the pain was by increasing my intake of *maconha* (marijuana). My new host family was super weird; besides having a tortoise wandering around the house without any sort of enclosure, my host mom would get angry when I "ate too much" and my host brother stared at me in the creepiest way imaginable. Toking regularly felt necessary to ease my anxiety. Luckily my fast best friend, Fernando, whom I met in my building, had an endless supply of terrible schwag weed—often *prensada* (compressed) and full of seeds and stems but eminently smokeable.

Fernando was super athletic like me, so we often ran together in the morning or evening. In the afternoon, we'd swim out to the boats docked in the famous Porto da Barra harbor beach at the end of our street—always with a few joints stashed in our snorkel masks so they wouldn't get drenched in the bay. His mom became my stand-in Brazilian mom—I still call her Tia Regina (Aunt Regina)—and their small home, decked out in Afro-Brazilian art, became my refuge. I quickly became close with Fernando's best friends Tainan and Grazy too. Tainan was earnest, agreeable, and often could be found in a cloud of smoke. Grazy's mom had just died, and she had fled her father, a diabetic alcoholic in the backwater interior of the state, to live with her aunt and cousins a few blocks from me in Salvador.

Grazy was also in a cycle of escaping her grief and learning to live in a new city, so we both felt fragile and in need of companionship. Even the initial language barrier didn't prevent us from quickly becoming attached at the hip. We called ourselves *cafe com leite*, coffee with cream, based on the contrast of her brown skin and jet black hair—emblematic of her indigenous roots—with my own pale features. She was patient with me as my Portuguese improved and gentle with my frequent cultural confusion. The two of us often could be found sunning on our local *praia*, dancing till dawn (or sometimes quite a few hours after) at music festivals, or laughing till we choked at juice shops around town.

I am forever grateful for Fernando, Tainan, and Grazy taking me under their wings. We palled around with a small group of fellow exchange students from my program throughout the week, but I spent every waking hour with these three Bahians. We had very little in common at the surface—they, a group of Afro-Brazilians and/or of indigenous descent, living in one of the poorest states in Brazil; me, a white girl with a privileged background from one of the richest countries in the world—but we ended up close to the point of siblings. They were with me through thick and thin. I spent some of the best months and most memorable moments of my life in Bahia with them—from backpacking trips, trekking through the small hippie villages of the Chapada Diamantina nature reserve; to doing cocaine for the first time in a porta potty at Carnaval. They also stuck by me in the hardest times, including after I was robbed at knifepoint on a deserted beach and when I contracted dengue fever.

I was bitten by an infected mosquito on a weeklong trip to Rio de Janeiro with my exchange program. I didn't start to show symptoms, though, until after landing in Brasília, where I'd gone to spend a few days with Fernando's family and Grazy over the Easter holiday. Since I had been out late dancing before my early morning flight out of Rio, we all assumed my initial fatigue when I landed in the country's capital was just due to sleep deprivation. But after a steady decline—involving a splitting headache, followed by rashes breaking out all over my body till my whole face turned as red as an *acerola*—I ultimately fainted. They took my limp body to a nearby state hospital before realizing they didn't have my health insurance information, so they provided the card of Fernando's friend Mariana instead. Her father was involved in the government, and they hoped his stature might fast-track me to a bed. When I woke up in the hospital, all the doctors were calling me Mariana and I figured I must have had a brain aneurysm and imagined this whole persona called Alicia. Talk about a mindfuck, on top of the most pain I've ever experienced coursing through my body.

My friends were eventually permitted to enter the room,

winking obviously and calling me Mariana so forcefully that I got the hint. My fever was so high at that point that I honestly didn't care what my name was. When I asked the doctor whether I'd be okay, he stoically responded that we'd have to wait to see whether or not my fever would become hemorrhagic—meaning I could bleed to death. Thankfully, my symptoms never progressed that far. I did end up with Bell's palsy—one side of my face drooping for days—and temporary nerve damage in the palms of my hands and soles of my feet, such that I felt pins and needles for some time after. The pain was so bad that I couldn't stand on my own, and Grazy had to skip her flight back to Bahia to take care of me. This included carrying me, crying like a child, into the shower to bathe me; her maternal instincts have always been strong.

During this ordeal, similarly to after my rape, I never contacted my parents to tell them about what I was going through. My exchange program eventually had to call and notify them that I hadn't returned to Bahia after our program trip to Rio de Janeiro and had been missing classes—assuring them that I was the most independent student they'd ever had and that I was surely off somewhere with my Brazilian friends and being well-taken-care-of (not entirely wrong). At that point, I filled in everyone involved with the most sparing details: I'd gotten sick but was on the mend and would be back to Salvador soon.

In hindsight, I know that my hyper self-reliance is a common trauma response, a coping mechanism learned from feelings of abandonment and helplessness experienced during childhood. I also imagine that because I suffered frequent violation of—and therefore detachment from—my own body as an intersex kid, I was more numb than I should have been to the new bodily harm I suffered through my rape and dengue infection. All I know is that I don't blame being in Brazil for any of it. Students suffer sexual assault far too frequently within our own borders, and mosquitos, ravenous for my "sweet blood," massacre me here as much as they did in South America. In fact, setting these incidents aside, I was happier during my six months in Bahia than I'd ever been in my two decades of life before. I had the opportunity to leave behind the person my family and doctors had always told me I was and live life on my own terms.

Besides the hippie surfer chick persona I cultivated by carrying around my friends' boards and smoking weed on the beach all day, I also experienced what it was like to be an outsider. As a blond girl in Salvador—a city that, at the time, was 54 percent mixed race and 29 percent Black—I lived as a visible "other" for the first time. Though I resembled the economically dominant class, I still stuck out like a sore thumb, which teaches you a lot. And living in a place like Bahia, where Afro-Brazilian culture is so evident in everyday life—from the citywide celebration of holidays dedicated to orixas (deities of Candomblé, an African religion, where each represents a force of nature) to the drum troupes parading weekly through the streets—showed me what life could look like when white, Western culture doesn't successfully stamp out traditions and displace bodies that don't match its hegemonic paradigm.

Given that Salvador was the original slave port of Latin America, I credit my placement in actual Bahian universities to gaining my first real understanding of slavery and its continued effect on society, in a way we don't gain through standard education in the US–except at historically Black colleges and universities (HBCUs). Unfortunately, current attacks on "critical race theory" across the United States mean this won't be improving anytime soon. I realize that had I not been thin, blond, and white, my experience immersing myself into a foreign society that struggles with racism as real as our homegrown version would have been very different. I'm grateful to have had six months to learn from professors and everyday residents of a region proudly defined by its Afro-Brazilian heritage.

When I had worked in restaurants in the past, where many of my fellow servers were Black and many of the kitchen workers were undocumented immigrants, I had felt that all of us executing the same side-work–polishing silverware and sweeping the floors–during our shifts was an equalizing experience. I'm embarrassed to say that it wasn't until my time in Brazil that I truly internalized the damage of colonialism or acknowledged my own white privilege. Even then, it took several years for me to become a "traitor to my race" on the home front, fighting to dismantle the systems that kept my privilege intact. And it would be many more years after that before I'd realize that these same forces of domination, bent on erasure of the "other," are what pathologized intersex bodies like mine in the first place.

I've returned to Salvador many times since my semester there; it's changed a lot but will always, in a sense, feel like home. On one trip back for a wedding, about eight years after I had packed up and moved out of that sacred city, I had a figa tattooed on the back of my neck. It symbolizes protection, which is what I've dedicated my life to securing for others. Intersex people bear the protection of those who struggled before us and fight for better protections for those who will come after. Inking the figa along the ridge of my spine is a permanent reminder of our struggle for safety and that the work neither starts nor ends with me.

Deciding to get this particular tattoo in Salvador itself was meaningful too. I experienced some of the worst trauma to my body during my first trip to Brazil, being assaulted outside of São Paulo and catching and recovering from dengue in Rio and Brasília. During my time in Salvador, though, I always felt truly safe and held by all I came in contact with—from the homeless residents on the beach, whom I came to know by name and who came to know me too, to my friends who healed me after assault and life-threatening illness. There are many phrases pertaining to Salvador da Bahia—from *sorría, você está na Bahia* (smile, you're in Bahia) to *é só alegria* (it's all good). It's a magical place that touches the soul of anyone who spends time there, and I'll always look back on my Bahian era through rose-colored glasses.

When I left Brazil, I was pretty depressed to return to Ithaca. Fortunately, I knew I had just one more year at Cornell. I focused my energy on landing a job after graduation and partying as hard as I could to get by until that day. I definitely made some lasting memories that year, from trying for the first time psyche-delic mushrooms—a plant medicine that has changed my life—to hooking up with my first famous musician (well, technically I had also made out with the lead singer of Rooney at the end of my senior year of high school, but I don't think he's exactly a household name, unless you watched *The O.C.* as fervently as my friends and I did). I will spare his identity for the sake of privacy, but he started his label in the city where I grew up. The night that this happened, he found me rapping in Portuguese in the kitchen of my friends' fraternity and started drumming along against the fridge, which was pretty epic.

What was less epic was having everyone on campus find out about it by the time I woke up the next morning—and the subsequent slut-shaming I then endured for months after. That morning, I rolled over in bed at the Statler—the on-campus hotel run by students in Cornell's hospitality school—and surveyed my work. *Damn; [insert name of world-renowned DJ] is drooling on the pillow next to me right now.* He woke up soon after, we exchanged numbers, and then we both departed, me to class and him to the airport. *Where the fuck is my wallet? Shit.* I dialed my friend Sam, who I knew wouldn't judge; you can rely on the gays to hype their girls after a salacious slam session. "I need to talk to you, STAT. Meet me at the engineering library where I work for the Annual Fund. It's midway between where I'm waking up right now and my apartment." Though it must have been 8 a.m., Sam sensed the urgency and dutifully agreed.

I sat on the low stone wall that lined the front steps of Carpenter Hall and whipped out a *cigarro de palha*—a small-farm tobacco cigarette wrapped in corn husk, which I'd started smoking during my time in Bahia and had my Brazilian friends continue to bring back for me after every trip they made home during school holidays. Sam approached and I extended the cigarette in his direction: "I think you're going to need a hit of this . . ."

I regaled him with the night's events, him shrieking with glee at every (in)appropriate detail, ending with how I had no idea where my wallet was. "My student ID and every other card I need to function is in that change purse," I told him through a puff of anxiety-ridden smoke.

"We'll figure that out and you can borrow my ID in the meantime," he said. "But first we need to take a moment to process that you just boned someone whose music you've had on repeat for the past four years. Let's appreciate this moment of queendom."

I smiled. Sam was right; this night had been one for the books. We parted ways and I headed home to shower off the previous twelve hours before sprinting to Environmental Econ. Entering the packed lecture hall, I caught multiple glances cast in my direction. *I guess I'm pretty disheveled?* I peered down through my glasses—I hadn't had time to put my contacts in—at the leggings and sweatshirt I'd hastily thrown on before running out the door. *No more than usual though... why is everyone looking at me?!* One girl distinctly looked my way and whispered to her neighbor, while another tapped something into her phone and showed it to the friend sitting next to her, who was staring unblinkingly in my direction. *Okay, shake it off. You're probably overtired and overthinking things.* But a quick trip to Libe Café for a much-needed jolt of caffeine after class confirmed my suspicions.

"Did you hear that Alicia Roth hooked up with [*world-renowned DJ*]?" I heard one student asking a friend seated across the table next to mine. Roth is my middle name and I used it—rather than my full name—on Facebook to help prevent potential employers from finding my photos online. *She obviously doesn't know who I am, or she wouldn't be talking about me right in front of my face.*

"Yeah," her friend replied. "What a ho." I choked on my iced mocha.

"Dan from Sig Chi texted me this morning—apparently it happened at an after-party at their annex."

"I guess they've been telling everyone," her friend said, displaying her phone screen to another student who'd just sat down to join them. "So embarrassing. She's going to have to lay low from parties for a while."

I share this story not just to flex on the fact that I had a thriving sex life in my twenties and spent some unforgettable nights with some pretty cool people I admire greatly. I also share it to show how a natural and healthy activity between two people can be so stigmatized, when a confident young woman is involved, that what should bring joy often gets squashed by shame. Had one of those fraternity members fucked a famous artist, he would have been the toast of the town. But when it's a female(-presenting) student in question, she's automatically branded the campus whore.

I had grown up ashamed of my body, thanks to trusted doctors and family members. Then, after having that body violated in Brazil, I was blamed into thinking it was my fault. Now, an act of pleasure had garnered me a scarlet letter I'd carry around for the rest of my time in Ithaca and in every cell of my body thereafter. I drank my way through the rest of the semester to numb the dark thoughts that accompanied this branding, but the layers of internalized shame I had accumulated by the time I reached adulthood were thick and heavy. I'd lug them around with me for years to come and am still working to shake them.

The tattoo on my neck reminds me to keep living, though, regardless of the haters; figas symbolize resistance too. Immersion in the communities that embraced me in Salvador was the first step onto my path of understanding our collective marginalization, as people whose bodies and cultures don't fit the dominant worldview, but also how we can revolt against it—through our struggle *and* our joy. The ink I got down in Salvador, and its placement, are a reminder to me and a warning to those who threaten us: as the late, great fellow Cornell alumna Ruth Bader Ginsburg once said, echoing the words of the nineteenth-century abolitionist and activist Sarah Moore Grimké, "I ask no favor for my sex. All I ask of our brethren is that they take their feet off our necks."

TAYSHAS

Tayshas means "friends and allies" in the language of the
Caddo tribes. Over the years and across a variety of tongues,
it evolved to "Tejas" and ended with what we now call Texas.
Though this state has been no friend to the allied groups that
first lived here, it's important to pay homage to our original
inhabitants as we form new bonds and build new communities.

TAYSHAS

After graduation, my very first nine-to-five job took me to New
York City—a magical land with plenty of other famous artists to
bag and far more anonymity to be able to avoid scrutiny for it.
I moved to a tiny spot in Brooklyn—East Williamsburg, if you're
a Realtor; Bushwick to everyone else—with the daughter of my
mom's friend and her roommate. It was in no way big enough
for the three of us. But cramming into an apartment straddled

between a White Castle and a housing project that I could barely afford on my paltry salary before (if) I started making a commission, with two grown-ups who'd been living in "the city" for years and had the hipster aesthetic to prove it—it was a dream. I was no longer stuck in a frigid small town with no nightlife to speak of besides chugging jungle juice from a fishbowl. The entire world was at my fingertips—so many friends to meet and allies to make.

My first job was also a pretty amazing opportunity for this wide-eyed recent college graduate. Selling sponsorship packages for tech conferences in Latin America meant that I had the opportunity to hobnob with C-level executives of enterprise-level companies in multiple countries and to travel frequently to enable me to do so. There were definitely a few hairy situations, in retrospect, when drunken businessmen got too handsy or "mistook" business dinners as opportunities to hit on me. One suited asshole even shook a wad of cash in my face, propositioning me, at a work event. At the time, though, all of this paled in comparison to the violation I'd experienced in Brazil. That, plus my naive barely twenty-two-year-old sensibility for what was or wasn't professional still hadn't registered that I didn't have to accept all this as "business as usual." I am grateful to have had a woman boss, Sara, who—I now understand in hindsight—not only fostered my professional growth but also protected me from a lot.

In spite of all this, I began dating one of my co-workers in secret soon after I started work. Steve was decently older and the most successful salesperson in our office, the Americas division of our global company. He was hyperinvolved in New York nightlife and the music scene, on every list at all the most fun under-ground venues, and friends with many of the DJs who played them. He is also one of the sweetest, funniest, and most enjoyable people I've ever dated, and I'm truly grateful to him for taking me under his wing and opening to me the world that is New York City. With Steve and his more seasoned crew often calling the shots, my close friends from college and I began to go out multi-ple nights a week to amazing dance clubs and warehouses—from Cameo Gallery to Le Bain to Output to Glasslands to SRB—most of which have since shuttered. We were often up dancing till sun-rise, at which point I'd take a disco nap followed by an Adderall and would stumble my way into the office, coffee in hand, a little closer to 9:30 a.m. than my boss would have liked.

The special musical moment we were part of, and the level of partying that accompanied it, just couldn't have sustained for-ever. My approximately two-year New York era was defined by a nu-disco sound and fueled by James Murphy's free time, given that LCD Soundsystem had "broken up" and he'd focused his energy on launching amazing acts through his DFA label—from YACHT to Holy Ghost! to Shit Robot.

After a year, I moved in with Jess, my best girlfriend from college. We found a relatively inexpensive building in the heart of Williamsburg that smelled of cigarette smoke and was full of some real characters who'd been in the neighborhood for decades if not generations. We proudly named our post-age stamp–size apartment the Disco Den. There was a hot pipe running through the middle of my room, which once melted the toe of one of my favorite pairs of boots, and I didn't have a closet. But we didn't care, the world was ours. That is, until one work trip to Brazil where Nathan happened . . .

Heading to São Paulo on business meant long days spent in the backseat of sweaty cabs, bopping from meeting to meeting to meeting across the largest city in Latin America. After work, I'd head to dinner and usually a club with some of my guy friends from college or girlfriends I'd met through them (I never again met with my original host family from my first stay in-country, as that would have involved dredging up memories I wasn't ready to face). Bella, in particular–a vivacious nerd who loved animals and *The Legend of Zelda*–had become my best friend in São Paulo, and her family essentially ended up adopting me as their third daughter. I'd often fly down early for work trips or extend them on the tail end to be able to stay with the Escobar family (no relation to Pablo . . . that we know of) and their nine dogs in the wealthy suburb of Alphaville.

By October 2013, I had begun to tire a bit of my relationship with Steve. As great of a guy as he was, it worried me that he still sustained a level of partying in his thirties that I was already tiring of at twenty-three. I was starting to awaken to the fact that I needed to feel some sense of purpose in life, beyond raking in commission for helping tech companies succeed and spending it on nights of debauchery. I didn't know where to find it yet, but I was starting to feel an ache for something else–something more. After wrapping my annual Brazilian conference that all those cabs and meetings culminated in, Bella wanted to take me out to meet her new boyfriend–a rich Paulista whom we referred to as a "playboy," which translates in both languages. She and I dressed up in our finest bandage skirts and heels to meet at a restaurant he invested in. He had also invited some friends and fellow business partners, and they were HOT. Long story short, I ended up drunkenly hooking up with his best friend, Nathan, later that night.

Waking up the next morning in my hotel was the guiltiest I'd felt since having to tell my ex, Mike, about my rape two and a half years before. This time, I hadn't been assaulted; I had consensually made out with another man on the dance floor—and in the parking lot—and in the Uber I ultimately called to take me back to where I was staying (before pushing him out and sending him on his way). Although we had only kissed, it was still cheating, and the worst part was that I wanted more. I had told Nathan I had a boyfriend; he knew it was complicated, but I woke up to a text message from him asking to take me on a date the following night. I also had a text from Bella that she and her boyfriend, Fernando, had broken up at the club, after we left, and she wanted my support. One door had closed while another opened.

Bella needed my help as she tearfully grasped for closure, so I packed my things to head to her family's home for the day. But Nathan and I had really connected at dinner, leading up to our transgressions, and he wanted to get to know me properly (sober) before I flew back to the States. He confirmed what I felt: something more than a one-night fling was there, so I accepted his invitation to at least head back into the city to see him later that night. The real litmus test was that when I told him I was planning to stay all the way out in Alphaville with Bella—more than an hour from the center of town—he still wanted to pick me up to take me to dinner and then home after. His willingness to endure hours of driving for one date seemed to solidify that this was worth giving a shot, regardless of the mess I'd have to clean up upon returning to New York.

The two-hour-long car rides we shared ended up being just the tip of the iceberg. After ending things with Steve back in NYC, I determined my time in that city was also meant to come to an end. I wanted more than an endless stream of parties, and at the time, it somehow felt like a city of twenty million people was just too small to escape the persona and livelihood I'd built with him there. I started to apply to jobs all across the States, in between subsequent business trips back to Brazil, where Nathan and I continued our dalliance. He was also trying to escape his current circumstances, never having left São Paulo and the friends and family he'd grown up with. Right when I received a job offer in San Francisco, he accepted one in France. This would put much more distance between an already geographically challenged situation, so he encouraged me to join him. I ended up pushing back my own job offer a month so I could meet him in Lyon first—a crazy and romantic notion but also an opportunity for us to be able to spend a significant chunk of time together, like a real couple, for the first time.

Moving into an ancient European flat in the Foch neighborhood, we embarked on this new adventure together, though not quite on equal footing. Nathan was working full time at his new job by the time I arrived and already spoke the language significantly better than my four years of elementary school classes afforded. Unlike *Emily in Paris*, I didn't have co-workers forced to interact with me on a daily basis. While I attempted to fill my days with cooking classes and runs along the Rhône, I also spent many lonely hours struggling to engage with locals who didn't want to entertain my rudimentary French or reading by myself in idyllic outdoor cafés. (Let me be clear: that now sounds like paradise. At the time, unhealed Alicia–still afraid of solitude and what she might have to face, left in the company of her own thoughts–hadn't yet realized how much of an introvert she actually is.)

I definitely have some great memories from that time–stuff that seems out of *The Lizzie McGuire Movie* or one of the Olsen twins' travel films from their teen years. Nathan and I managed to eat at all of "Chef of the Century" Paul Bocuse's restaurants in our home base of Lyon. We also took frequent weekend trips that involved experiences like taking a horse-drawn carriage to see one of my favorite artists, Nicolas Jaar, perform in a warehouse on an island in the middle of a park in Munich. Amidst all the fantasy, though, a reality ultimately set in that my relationship with Nathan perhaps wasn't as sustainable as I thought (a foreign man I cheated on my prior boyfriend with? Shocker!). He was more interested in my having dinner ready on the table–or waiting in lingerie, or ideally both–when he arrived home from work than he was in connecting with me at a deeper level that I needed to keep moving things forward, in what would have then become an intercontinental affair.

Not having found the meaning I was searching for in a Brazilian dude in France, I left for San Francisco to build a new life focused on work, rather than on parties and men. The only issue was that I hated my job. On the basis of my relationships with tech companies in Latin America, I'd been brought on to manage Apple's affiliate marketing programs in the region—seated in a large and well-reputed advertising firm that had just won the company as a client. I was quickly promoted and started rising through the ranks in what most people saw from the outside as a dream job. But there were two main barriers to bliss, constantly bringing me back to a less fortunate reality. First, I was supposed to get folks excited about updates like the next iPhone model being a millimeter thinner, when *I* didn't care about an iPhone becoming a millimeter thinner. It's hard to evangelize about something you just aren't excited about. This issue was easier to swallow and push aside, however—as more money and higher titles were offered—than the straw that ultimately broke the camel's back . . .

I was working in the San Francisco office of a New York–based company, one that first arose from the Madison Avenue advertising boom. If you've watched *Mad Men*, you know that the culture epitomized by Don Draper's character is not exactly centered on women's empowerment. And you might not be surprised to learn that way less has changed during the more than half century after the show was set than one would have hoped. Although my direct boss was a woman (and another badass one, like I was blessed with at my first job out of school), none of her bosses were women. The head of our division was a winning combo of absent and incompetent, and his higher-ups seemed content with accommodating these shortcomings. And the person he ultimately reported to—one of the chief ranking officers of the agency nationally—was known for getting too drunk at holiday parties or company outings and becoming progressively forward toward women employees. To drop the euphemisms: he frequently and blatantly harassed his subordinates, and the company continually hushed it up, at best, or joked about it, at worst. "Oh, you know Howie" was a common chuckle among the men who signed my paychecks. I *did* know him, and I didn't like it.

Miserable, at this point, in my daily routine (curating a rotating assortment of oatmeal toppings was the honest-to-God highlight of my eight-to-six days), I needed an outlet. Beyond the trail running and concert-going I'd established in earlier life phases, I threw myself into a new extracurricular activity: the now defunct women's network formerly known as Spark. Before Spark joined forces with Global Fund for Women, its members helped steward more than $1.7 million in funds to ninety organizations in thirty-five countries, serving more than forty thousand women and girls globally. Being a part of this work was exhilarating in a way I'd never felt professionally.

At the end of most work days, I'd hustle out of the office and straight to meetings of Spark's Investment Committee, Vetting Committee, Fundraising Committee, Marketing Committee— whatever I could sink my teeth into. Over pizza and soda, we'd evaluate the applications of nonprofits worldwide, select which we felt had the most promise, and strategize the best ways to support them through raising money and providing pro bono consulting. Funneling funds into free coding boot camps for survivors of human trafficking got me out of bed in the morning, where newly launched shades of the iPod Shuffle couldn't. I lived for this social change "work," but I didn't make a living from it; *that* had to change.

In order to move forward, I looked back. An excerpt from a blog post I wrote at the time reads:

Following my time in Brazil and a period of extreme reverse culture shock, I resumed my "normal" life, but have never been quite the same. I graduated from Cornell, worked corporate jobs in two of the most exciting cities the US has to offer, learned a lot, saved a little, and have led a life that the majority of the world's twenty-somethings would be envious of. I have no complaints and, with a few exceptions, nothing but positive memories.

That being said, there is a difference between contentment and fulfillment. I've mastered sales, digital marketing, and other invaluable skills. I've forged partnerships, managed subordinates, and served a variety of roles within local and global teams.

So what am I lacking?

As my LinkedIn endorsements continue to grow, my own personal success evaluators—the aforementioned feelings of "fascinated," "challenged," and "accomplished"—have not followed suit.

I needed to reignite my sense of wonder and committed to do so in the way I knew best: travel.

Backpacking across the Southern Cone of South America over my Christmas holiday, a girlfriend of mine from California and I crossed paths with a jovial group of locals in Punta del Este—the Miami of Uruguay, to paint it in reductive but comparative terms. Juan Pablo, the rowdiest of the lot, and I quickly hit it off and ended up making out under the fireworks that rang in 2015. He offered to take me to Cabo Polonio the next morning—a seaside fishing village with no power or running water, accessible only by dune buggy—which seemed like a better way to start the year than writhing in bed hungover with the rest of our crew. We stole away in secret, only to be soaked to the skin by torrential downpours in the open-air cart ferrying us over the dunes. As I sat shivering, nursing a beer by the bonfire outside of a simple surf shack once we arrived, I knew it wasn't just from the cold . . . I felt it again—that inexplicable electric current running through my veins that I hadn't plugged into since Salvador.

Juan Pablo no longer lived in this tiny country, dwarfed by its giant neighbor where I'd first caught my mojo during my semester abroad. He worked in the automotive industry and had found a lucrative job in Angola—where I spoke the national language of Portuguese and where he had an extra bedroom. Laying my soul bare to him in that surreal place, I shared my real yearning for more in my life. *More of what?* I wasn't sure, and I certainly didn't know where to find it. He suggested finding an excuse to go to West Africa for a bit, to stay with him while I figured it out. That electrical current sparked. *What if I leaned into the spark—and Spark—by leaving my job, subsisting on my savings for a bit, and volunteering with organizations we funded through Spark's network?* It seemed crazy and definitely was not something that would fit easily on LinkedIn. It did seem *fascinating*, though, and *challenging*, for sure. If I hadn't found the sense of *accom-*

plishment I sought on the corporate ladder, maybe I wasn't going to find it in California either.

Upon returning to the States, I promptly gave notice at my job and started packing up the room in my apartment in Cole Valley. As I rode out the end of my formal employment, I hustled to expedite visas to a variety of African countries where I had friends through school and work connections. Once secured, I booked a flight to Luanda, where Juan Pablo lived.

The day before I was set to fly out, he called to notify me that he'd been kicked out of the country and had one week to vacate. *Shit.* *But* Juan Pablo had a group of Portuguese friends from work who'd be sticking around and who had extra bedrooms galore—a silver lining, maybe bronze. He assured me that, on the basis of what he'd told them about me, they were all willing to host me in his stead—"Any friend of Juan Pablo's is a friend of ours!"—so he recommended I come spend a few days with him and then determine whether any of his buds would make viable longer-term hosts for after his departure.

Cross an ocean to stay with a guy I barely knew, who was being expelled from his country of residence for some unexplained reason, before moving in with complete strangers in a region I'd never been to? My current self wants to smack twenty-something Alicia across the head—okay, something less violent but equally forceful—to knock some sense into her. But I'd taken the sensible path for too long at that point, from the Ivy League school where I wasn't happy to the corporate job that didn't fit. If I didn't hop off that path soon, I was afraid I never would. The "logical" conclusion was to take the plunge across the pond. Luckily, Juan

Pablo's friends ended up being way cooler than he was and fast became my brothers from a Portuguese mother. They took care of me, buying groceries on their salaries and paying for dinners when we dined out. These platonic sugar daddies enabled me to evaluate a local nonprofit, Plataforma Mulheres em Acção (PMA), for Spark funding and to "study" for my Foreign Service Officer Test—the excuse I'd given to everyone back stateside for what I'd be focusing my energy on next. For my Tuga—colloquial for mainland Portuguese—crew, I am still very grateful.

I lucked out and didn't end up in a ditch on the side of a road, or the victim of some gringa-smuggling ring (either of those could have been very real possibilities, as I soon learned upon landing). Angola was, and is, unlike anywhere else this wide-eyed white girl had ever been or has been since. I quickly received a crash course in some harsh realities...

First, the reason I couldn't afford groceries or meals out there is because an after-dinner drink alone once cost us $75 USD; in a famous case, a French resident had to pay $105 USD for a single melon. Most of what *would* be farmable land across the country is ridden with land mines, following four decades of armed conflict—for which, by the way, the US furnished weapons and munitions in our Cold War efforts to eradicate the global "communist threat" and to gain influence over Angolan oil. While we and primarily the Chinese siphoned off the country's oil, it had to import most everything else, unable to grow sufficient food amidst the hidden explosives.

You'd never learn it in the majority of American history books, but our sustained, multigenerational support of colonial systems continues to starve the Global South. Meanwhile, our expats profit off of its natural resources, in Angola's case, oil. Never have I seen so many Texans outside of Texas as during my time in Luanda. But since there is little diversification of industry beyond petroleum, and since nearly everything needed for survival must be brought in from elsewhere, the prices of food and other everyday items are absurd—jacked up to levels that justify the cost of importing those goods for a relatively small group of buyers, the foreign and domestic oil elite. At the time I was there, the average Angolan made $2 USD a day and could not afford safe or sufficient food—subsisting mainly on "poxo" porridge (flour mixed with water)—let alone shoes or proper hygiene.

We passed children bathing in trash-filled roadside ditches daily, while my Portuguese friends' kids lived securely in gated compounds with more amenities than I've ever seen in the States. Income inequality is a reality in most of the modern world, and certainly here at home, but what I witnessed in Luanda was stark. Global inequality is most often measured by an index called the Gini coefficient; per this index, Angola was ranked thirteenth in the world for its gap between rich and poor the year I wrote this book (the US ranked fifty-third). I imagine the disparity was even worse when I was there, two years before they ousted their then "president" after more than thirty-seven years in power.

The reality of my Portuguese friends' choosing to live in Angola is rife with colonial dynamics *and* also complicated by the fact that they were escaping high levels of joblessness in their own country—the unemployment rate nearly three times then what it is today and over ten times more than what we currently suffer in the US. I also couldn't have afforded to stay there on my own. But the fact that I was there in the first place was a problem.

While I came armed with a degree focused on international political economy in the developing world, I also came bearing a white feminist lens to my approach to solving problems. I had arrived with the intention of evaluating local PMA leadership for Spark investment, only to realize that I felt unqualified to do so—not because of any inadequacy in my academic preparation but rather because of my lack of local context and community involvement. Cloistered in a gated community built and funded by those taking Angola's resources, I felt more insecure than ever in my right to make decisions on how to best solve problems I was inadvertently contributing to.

I feel it's important to recognize my own insertion into the problematic power structures of international development. The fact that I wasn't able to recognize this until I was physically in a recipient country is a problem too, demonstrating the lack of empathy and real global understanding that we inculcate into white Americans. This is reinforced by institutions like our educational system but also by each of us refusing to critically examine our own selves and sometimes call ourselves out, or in.

Rather than remain paralyzed by inertia on the distribution of Spark funding, however, I chose to pivot to blogging about what I saw and sharing some of these dynamics to help at least try to educate other Western women in my sphere of influence back at home. I know I did open some minds on the home front, but I also put myself in danger on the ground. My friend Rafael Marques de Morais, an Angolan journalist and human rights defender focused on investigating government corruption, was protected by his international notoriety—he was too visible to be "disappeared" by the government without foreign fallout. But I was, at the time, a no-name rogue blogger. My mother urged me to register with the Committee to Protect Journalists; the diplomats I hung out with in Luanda reminded me that in reality, organizations like that could do very little for me in the event I were to be disappeared.

On the basis of this fear, my discomfort with living in luxury in a failed state, and my feelings of inadequacy to provide the PMA's leadership with valuable support, I decided pretty quickly that my stay in Angola should not and would not be extensive. I wrote to a friend from home living in (relatively) nearby South Africa to ask whether I might stay with her for a bit, while I figured out next steps, and booked a flight to Cape Town.

Packing my things in a hurry, I also tucked away many great memories I'd managed to make in such a short time—from island trips and beach camping, to spending the night in the French Embassy on my last night in the country (with someone I won't identify but who worked in that building). I was sad to leave many great friendships behind, not only with my Portuguese hosts but also with a handful of Angolan women I'd managed to meet and befriend along the way. But I was ready to head to a place where I felt I could meaningfully contribute to solutions, not just to problems.

Moving from tropical Angola to chilly South Africa was jarring in a variety of ways. Beyond a temperature change for which I had woefully underpacked, I'd no longer be staying in a gated community but rather in an apartment I shared with six other students in Observatory—then a still largely ungentrified neighborhood near the University of Cape Town. I'd be working in this same community too. My friend Elspeth, with whom I stayed upon first arriving, had highly recommended I evaluate a local organization for Spark funding called Sex Workers Education and Advocacy Taskforce (SWEAT). This was long before "sex work is work!" chants became normalized at women's rights rallies or before feminism had more broadly accepted the ideas of decriminalization into its platform. I began my fellowship with the org rife with biases though committed to learn. (For those who haven't yet caught up: if the government shouldn't be policing what folks do with their uterus, then they shouldn't be telling folks what to do with their vagina either—or any orifice, for that matter.)

My spring and summer at SWEAT proved to be the most transformative experience in my tenure as an activist to that point. First off, I was seated in the organization's Advocacy and Networking program, which enabled me to utilize my privilege as a white woman and member of the international community to lift up the activism sex workers already were engaging in— helping them access platforms that wouldn't usually be afforded to one of the communities most marginalized by society. I also wrote grants to help bring in funding to fuel sex workers' efforts to demand rights and provide mutual aid.

During my tenure, members of the organization were hyperfocused on the trial of a famous artist, Zwelethu Mthethwa, who had murdered their friend and fellow sex worker Nokuphila Kumalo. Though there was CCTV footage of him stomping her to death on a street corner in 2013, it was four years before a verdict was reached in 2017. Society strips sex workers of their humanity, and Mthethwa—rich enough to drive a custom Porsche in the most unequal country in the world—had lawyered up with the best scumbag defense attorney money could buy.

I spent my energy supporting, in one of two ways, the state-appointed prosecutor who represented the deceased and her surviving mother. By day, I attended gallery openings, exhibits, and other networking events within Cape Town's art community to dig up dirt on the man who had killed Kumalo. At night, I accompanied SWEAT's workers for drop-offs of safe sex materials such as condoms and lube at brothels and on street corners, where we often also found witnesses and evidence for the trial. In addition, I got to witness and participate in some of the most amazing community-building initiatives, led by and for sex workers, I've ever seen—from prayer circles to educational seminars to makeshift communal childcare. I also learned some of the best organizing techniques, which I still utilize today, at their rallies outside of the Cape Town High Court, where I helped garner media visibility for the trial.

My friends, who happened to be sex workers, embraced me into their world, despite all our differences. They had no idea I was intersex, a member of a community pushed almost as far to the margins of society as theirs, and was also struggling for my own body autonomy; I hadn't even internalized any of that yet myself. They simply saw me as a fellow human with an imperfect understanding of the world but a willingness to hear and share their stories and an interest in helping however I could. They taught me so much, not just about effective advocacy but other vital skills—such as how to tell aggressive men to fuck off in Afrikaans, Zulu, and Xhosa—as well as less tangible stuff, such as how empathy really is a galvanizing force. To put it directly, I have learned more about activism, feminism, and life from Black and brown, trans, and homeless sex workers than any other group.

I was able to cover my bills for a time through a combination of a wild exchange rate that took my savings way further than would have been possible in most other countries and some odd jobs I worked while I was there. (Perhaps the oddest, yet coolest, was recording voice-overs in Portuguese for a company that provided subsidized fire detection systems in townships where most of my friends from SWEAT lived.) I also spent some of the last dollars in my bank account touristing in nearby Namibia and Mozambique, two of the most beautiful places I've ever seen. The African continent is completely misunderstood by the majority of Americans, who buy in to a poorly painted picture that distills so many places and cultures into a reductionist sliver of what can be found there.

Not all that I saw in Africa was poverty and strife. Before leaving the continent, I also had the luxury of swimming with whale sharks and great whites, hiking mountains at sunrise, and sliding into pools filled with wine at sunset (the Robertson Wine Valley's Wacky Wine Weekend truly is wild). I danced at some clubs I wish we could replicate stateside, discovering passions for kuduro and Nigerian dancehall that rival my love of reggaeton—well, almost. Speaking of love, I also dated yet another Brazilian dude (whom I met at the base of Table Mountain but who was actually friends with my ex I spent time with in France, weirdly enough) and someone from South Africa too. After less than a year in southern Africa, though, I'd eaten through way more of what I'd saved from my former career in tech than I'd originally planned.

Needing the stability of a traditional paycheck more than more adventures at that point, I headed back to California in September 2015 for a new job that would leverage both my prior experience in marketing and new skills in community organizing. Joining the team at Fenton to run social change campaigns was almost like enrolling in a fraternity of change-makers; the company has churned out some of the best in the biz, across issue areas and over the course of decades, who've gone on to serve movements in a variety of communications capacities and otherwise. I also credit my colleagues there with pulling me left of center and helping me truly understand social justice (it was during this time that I attended my first Black Lives Matter protest—sprinting into oncoming traffic to help shut down Interstate 880 in July 2016). I knew this job would be a great stepping stone but also that I had no desire to be back in the Bay Area for long.

I stayed most of this second stint in California in the city of Oakland. I much preferred it to its neighbor San Francisco, where I'd lived before my foray into the Eastern Hemisphere. The East Bay, though perhaps less picturesque than SF, is more diverse. Plus, at least at that time it hadn't yet been saturated by the tech bros who'd already claimed the land across the bay. I enjoyed living in the neighborhood of Temescal, where I contributed to a tight-knit community. My neighbors and I shared resources: Luke had chickens, Ben grew veggies, I had pomelo trees in the backyard, and Johnny distilled his own absinthe and made silao berry wine. We never called ahead to see if someone was home, preferring just to stroll over and knock on the door.

I spent my free time after work with them and playing percussion in a band called Maracatu Pacifico, which borrowed a musical style from the northeast of Brazil, not far from where I'd studied abroad. On the weekends, I enjoyed camping or shucking oysters in the beautiful surrounding region with my San Francisco friends. It wasn't perfect—I sometimes had safety concerns, including a shoot-out on my block one afternoon— but it was honestly pretty idyllic. After my year traipsing Africa, though, my life back stateside included almost *too* much ease; I was ready for my next challenge.

A couple years before, while I was still living in New York, a former Texas state senator, Wendy Davis, had become famous for what's now known as the People's Filibuster. Wendy, wearing her now famous pink tennis shoes, spoke for thirteen hours straight on the Texas Senate floor to help kill a bill that would have severely restricted abortion access across the state. She was not allowed to sit, lean, stop to pee, or drink water for the duration of her speech, which included personal testimonies from people who'd had abortions in all corners of the state.

As the Texas State Legislature had just adopted the technology to support live-streaming these sorts of hearings, political junkies watched on the edge of their seats from across the country and around the world. So many supporters ended up cramming their way into the Capitol building and shouted so loud that legislators were ultimately unable to take a voice vote by the necessary deadline for the bill to pass. This discriminatory piece of legislation died at midnight, and the moment lives forever in the memories of Texans on both sides of the aisle.

Although I hadn't yet set foot in the state that gave me my name, I'd heard about Wendy's leadership in this historic instance. As any self-respecting feminist would be, I was obsessed. When she ultimately ran for governor, was painted as "abortion Barbie," and lost, she decided to take some time out of public office to train the next generation of young women activists in the Lone Star State. Having never run a nonprofit before, Wendy came to speak with the executive director of Spark–who was, by this point, well-known for supporting early-stage women-led orgs worldwide. She requested advice on how to launch what she'd be calling Deeds Not Words, after the original suffragette motto.

At that point, her organization was simply an internet landing page that read "Deeds Not Words, coming soon" followed by a contact form. When Amanda, Spark's executive director, bragged to the rest of us about how she had advised Wendy, I immediately went to the site and spilled my life story and love for Wendy's work into the fields of the form.

I never expected to hear back from such a booked-and-busy icon, so when a member of her team reached out to me out of the blue a few months later to schedule a Skype meeting, I thanked my lucky stars. After just a half hour of glitchy online conversation, both Wendy and I knew our connection was special. She, having grown up in a southern trailer park, and me, having been a private school student in the Northeast–well, it would seem we had very little in common. But as two Tauruses who didn't take "no" for an answer, blond women who'd been underestimated our whole lives, and humans who cared above all else about making the world a better place, we saw a lot of ourselves in each other.

She told me, "I'm looking for a game-changing apprentice, as the job description I sent you puts it, to learn from me and support me as we build a pathway for women looking to follow in my footsteps, and I think you could be that person." She continued, "You've been back in California only a year, though—are you sure you're ready to relocate from the bluest to the reddest state? Would you at least want to come visit and check out Austin first?"

"I moved to Angola, sight unseen," I replied. "This is way less scary than that! I'm ready."

Little did I know, after all that bouncing around—from job to job, country to country—Texas would be the place to suck me in and keep me. In retrospect, I attribute part of my frenetic wandering to early signs of mania—a symptom of yet another major diagnosis that I wouldn't receive for a few more years and certainly didn't recognize at the time. (If it was hard to keep up reading this past chapter, just imagine my struggle trying to declare a place of residence to receive mail or claim sources of income for tax purposes.) I also credit this placelessness to the fact that I'd been searching for something—across various decades, industries, and continents—that I ultimately had to find within myself.

If you'd told this now self-proclaimed feminist—who'd lived most of her life on the coasts—that she'd end up working in Deep South politics, even a few months before making this last and final move, I probably would have laughed in your face. It's funny too to think that a deeply suppressed intersex person was on the verge of finally finding the peace she sought in this seemingly most hostile of places. But things were about to get even harder before they got better. Moving to the Lone Star State in October 2016, just weeks shy of that catastrophic presidential election, conditions in the region—and across the whole world—were about to shift very drastically for the target audience of our work...

The Caddo people of Texas had originally banded together as *tayshas* to fight off invading regimes like the French and Spanish. Through Deeds Not Words, we were about to have to build a hell of a coalition ourselves to fight off the Trumpism that was spreading across the state and country like cancer and was about to take hold. The lessons I'd learned building friends and allies across the globe—running events in Brazil, building partner networks in California, organizing communities in Africa, and forging online social change hubs back in the Bay Area—were all about to come into play. But if I was going to be fighting with and for new communities in the South, I had to recognize those who originally fought for their freedom on this land.

Tayshas, my first tattoo, sits on my rib cage above my heart. I got it in my hometown of Philadelphia, with my best friend from childhood, soon after putting down roots in my new home. Though I'd moved six times over the previous five years, something about this move felt permanent; the choice to get inked reflected that. When I told my friend and everyone else I cared about that after all my bouncing around, I intended to settle in Texas, they all thought I was insane; maybe I was. I was determined to change the world but had no idea how much my own world would change upon moving to Austin. Things were—as we so proudly tout here in the capital city—about to get weird.

BRIDGE

Build bridges, not walls.

Hurricane Alicia landed back in Texas, and Wendy Davis picked me up at the airport. I'd told her I was fine taking the subway, as most of my things would be arriving separately with movers in a few days, and she cackled. "Oh honey, there's no subway in Austin. Welcome to Texas!" Indeed. After loading my checked bag and carry-on into the trunk of her huge car, I was struck by how small the woman at the wheel was. Someone with a presence that powerful seemed bigger in my imagination.

Wendy pointed out landmarks and talked me through the vibes of various neighborhoods as we drove along, serving as my first tour guide in the new city I'd be calling home. We stopped at the light on Cesar Chavez and Congress Avenue and she gestured down the avenue. "Look right and you'll catch the Capitol a few blocks down—we'll be spending a whole lot of time there. And if you look left, you'll see the famous South Congress Bridge. Over a million bats fly out from under it every night in the spring and summer." I'd end up getting this same bridge tattooed on my ankle a couple of years later.

When Wendy hired me, she'd put out a call to her prior campaign networks to let them know she had a new staffer moving to town who could use a place to stay as she got her bearings. "Supporter housing" is a pretty common concept in the political world, as young professionals often move to new cities to work a campaign for short stints. Since their salaries are covered by campaign contributions (read: very low), sometimes donors choose instead to put one up in a spare bedroom to help ease costs to the candidate. In my case, one of Wendy's donors had a whole spare apartment, and she'd agreed to let me stay a couple of months till I got on my feet. "I've stayed in this spot before, and it's super nice," Wendy told me, as we pulled into the parking garage of a high-rise downtown. "You can also walk to Whole Foods across the street, which will be helpful till you get a car. You certainly won't be able to afford a place like this on your salary, so don't get too used to it!" She laughed.

As it turned out, this building was the first high-rise ever built in the city. At the time, the neighbors tried to kill the project because they were worried about the shadow it might cast over the single-family neighborhoods in nearby West Austin. White, wealthy residents protesting new development in a growing city? Who would've thought! Anyway, the building was also fancy, as Wendy mentioned, with a slew of doormen, including Tarek and Roderick, with whom I became close over the course of my stay. Then there was the late-night guard, whose name I didn't know but who often wore South African army regalia, only intensifying the creepy vibes he gave off. I'd often sit and hang in the lobby with Roderick or Tarek on my way in or out of the building, when I had time. When getting home late from the bars, however, I'd give the night guard a quick "hello" in passing before booking it to the elevator.

My first weeks in the building were an exhilarating yet exhausting whirlwind. Not only was I cycling to and from our office on the East Side every day on a bike Wendy gifted me, but I was also taking advantage of Austin's famous nightlife, accepting every personal and professional invitation to build my network in a new city. As I arrived home, sweaty and beat at the end of one of my first days in town, a bouquet of roses awaited me at my doorstep. *That's weird*, I thought, looking for a note but finding none. *No one has my address here besides Mom and Wendy . . . must be a happy mistake.* But when more arrived again the next day, and the next, and the next, I started getting a bit concerned. Sometimes a note accompanied the flowers, but it was always vague—"Beauty for beauty" or something to that effect—and the card was never signed. After almost a week of these nightly deliveries, I decided to let Wendy know.

"You're sure you didn't give any guys your address?" she asked, visibly concerned. "I'm sure you've had plenty of suitors since you arrived." She wasn't wrong, but I hadn't had anyone over. I was currently preoccupied by another long-distance fling with yet another Brazilian—this time, one of my guy friends from college whom I'd recently hooked up with at another one of their weddings in Mexico. He was currently living in Paraguay and assured me he wasn't sending me flowers but that he could, if I sent him my address. (As a side note, he has since passed and I miss him dearly; *que a alma dele descanse em paz.*)

"No one knows where I'm living," I confirmed. "I tried calling the flower company, and they told me that the recipient address is correct but they can't legally tell me who's sending them."

"Give me their number and I'll take care of it," Wendy replied, her voice somber. "A man who broke into my house while I was sleeping during my gubernatorial race just got out of jail, and I'm worried that maybe he's found out your connection to my work and is trying to get to me." I was now alarmed. "If they won't tell me who's sending them, we'll get the police involved, but I can be pretty convincing."

When I arrived at the office that day, a bouquet awaited me. Panicked, I tore open the note: "Congrats on the new gig, badass! We miss you here already, —Calisa." I immediately called Calisa, my old boss in San Francisco, who confirmed that she had not sent any of the other flowers and was sad to hear that her gift had not brought me joy but rather more stress. "Thank you so much for sending them!" I told her. "They really are beautiful. Oh wait, Wendy's calling me back so I gotta go . . ."

Wendy explained that after a particularly stern phone call with the flower company, she had managed to get the name of the person who'd been sending the bouquets: Stoffel Maiburg.

Sounded vaguely South African but didn't ring a bell as anyone I'd known while living there. After searching for the name on the internet, the image that popped up seared into my brain: the late-night doorman from my building. I immediately biked home and relayed the information to an irate Tarek, who put in a request for a meeting with building management the next morning to report the issue. In the meantime, I pushed a heavy couch against the door to the apartment while I slept (the front desk retained copies of every apartment key).

Arriving at the office of the building manager, Johannes, the next morning, I registered from his accent that he was also an Afrikaner—or white South African—like Maiburg. After repeating an abridged version of the account Tarek had reported, I was shocked by the manager's reply: "You're just a guest in the building—so our usual policies governing matters between building staff and residents don't apply in this scenario." He took a breath before continuing, "But I have spoken with Mr. Maiburg and he referenced that you've always been extremely friendly to him, giving him the impression that you might appreciate such a gesture."

At this point my mouth fell open. "I'm sorry," I said, "but because I'm polite enough to say 'hello' to someone I pass by multiple nights a week—someone who is paid to help me feel safe—that opens the door [pun intended] for him to start sending me creepy, anonymous gestures of affection that remind me he knows exactly where I live?!"

Johannes's smile lessened. "I'll let him know that you would not like to receive any more flowers, and I'd recommend that you no longer communicate with him as you enter the building while he's on shift."

For all I knew, Johannes could have been one of Maiburg's army buddies from back in South Africa. I decided to rise from my seat and leave. As I let the door to his office shut behind me, I realized I would never feel safe again in a building where Maiburg sat with his holstered gun, in his army fatigues, retaining a copy of my keys at hand. It was time to expedite the process of searching for a new place to live.

In the meantime, I had a few friends over to partake in a ritual with me that evening. I had saved all the flowers as "evidence," had the incident ended up being related to Wendy's old stalker. We carried them down to the pool late that night, after Maiburg had returned to his post, and dumped them in it. It looked like a scene from a horror movie—bloodred flowers scattered across the water, floating macabrely in the moonlight. I knew he could see all that we did through his security camera, and although the act was little more than symbolic, it felt significant. Yes, he'd sent anonymous flowers, not death threats. But I needed him to know the gesture was not well-received.

Women everywhere will understand a few aspects of what happened here. First, the simple act of kindness and cordiality—saying "hello" as I entered and left the building—being mistaken as a kind of advance. Second, the act of being hit on by someone in a situation where it's absolutely inappropriate. Third, feeling afraid in places we deserve to feel safe. Fourth, not being taken seriously when reporting misconduct. The fact that this happened immediately upon starting my new full-time career in gender equity only underscored the importance of the work Wendy and I were embarking upon. That it happened just about a week before Donald Trump was elected into the highest office of our land—even after all the misogynistic and outright dangerous information released about his own actions—underscored the urgency of getting that work done.

I think anyone who respects women remembers the sinking feeling as each new state's results rolled in the night of the election, culminating in a rock bottom when we realized that our worst fears had come true. Through hot tears, I texted Wendy at 11:41 p.m.:

I don't know what to do.

We get back up. And we fight back strong.

OK . . . I'm ready.

Waking up in that room, where I already didn't feel safe, the morning after the election was one of my bleakest moments. I caught myself in the mirror. I was still in my campaign T-shirt, and Hillary's stylized red-and-blue face stared back at me. Glancing up at my own, I registered the empty feeling reflected in my eyes, which had since changed from tear-swollen to hollow. But Wendy's words—so resolute, even at this darkest hour—stuck with me. We had set out to train girls to value and use their voices at a much younger age than when we'd learned to do so, hoping that by the time they reached my age, a world where someone like Trump could become president would no longer exist.

I cried again as I began to pack my things, resolved to channel my grief into finding a new home faster than originally planned. I needed to feel safe—or as safe as was possible, under our new Cheeto in Chief—in order to envision a society where all women could feel safe. I moved into a small Austin bungalow in the nearby neighborhood of Bouldin Creek with a couple of room-mates and put blinders on to focus on just that.

I poured every ounce of myself into building the Deeds Not Words organization from the ground up and finding meaningful ways for women, girls, and allies of all ages to plug in. We ran newsletters and online action campaigns offering Daily Deeds for followers across the country who, like me, had fallen under Wendy's spell since the filibuster. But what meant the most to me was our in-person work with the community through our campus training programs.

We identified and engaged with high schools and colleges across Central Texas, teaching students as young as thirteen how to shape their futures through legislative advocacy. Our goal was not just to help young women better understand the political process—filling in gaps in civic education in schools, which is sorely lacking—but also to guide them through generating some tangible wins. The sensation of winning was important; by tast-ing what it feels like to achieve a real goal via clearly defined steps, they would learn to truly believe in their own power and gain faith in certain mechanisms available to help them claim it. We hoped that by funneling them into these processes early, our student activists might one day end up launching their own organizations, running for political office, or at least becoming lifelong voters. We also knew it was vital to meet them where they are, so our first meetings with students became a listening tour to figure out which issues were most important to them.

If you asked young folks now what they considered to be the most important issues, the answer would likely vary but fall heavily on climate change and its disproportionate impact on certain populations, as influenced by environmental racism. But in 2017, the nationwide Women's Marches after Trump's inauguration had become the largest single-day protest in US history, and issues of bodily autonomy weighed heavy on young minds. Many of our college-age students were survivors of sexual assault themselves; all of our students, high school and older, personally knew someone who was. And some of the high schools we worked with had completed a curriculum developed by a nonprofit called Nest, which empowers youth as leaders in the eradication of sexual violence against children. Equipped with intervention skills to ensure their friends wouldn't get groomed into systems of exploitation, our students felt that fighting sex trafficking was a priority for them too.

Weirdly enough, both of these issues were also priorities for the Republican-majority Texas State Legislature that year. To understand why, I have to nerd out for a sec . . . Texas is a huge-ass state, second largest in the US, in both size and population. Back before the age of planes, trains, and automobiles, legislators would have to take their horses and buggies or whatever all the way from whichever far-reaching corner of the state they lived in to the capital city of Austin to meet with their fellow legislators and pass laws. Given that that journey could be well over five hundred miles and include snakes, mountain lions, diphtheria, and all the other hazards we remember from playing *Oregon Trail*, it made sense to consolidate all their legislating into a set period of time, called a session. They decided to host a legislative session every two years so they could bust out a bunch of laws for six months together and then travel back home to spend the rest of the time tending to their farms and families—and theoretically engaging with their constituents to better understand the issues they should be fighting to resolve during their next Austin tenure.

The Texas constitution maintains this same system to this day, almost two centuries after the first session was held. And kinda like how a certain party idealizes loyalty to the original piece of paper that counted Black Americans as three-fifths of their white counterparts, Texas Republicans are in no hurry to change things. Because cramming two years of governance into six months entails legislators working at all hours (I've spoken at bill hearings at 2 a.m., 4 a.m., even 6 a.m.) seven days a week, it's harder for the public to keep tabs on what's happening. The senators and reps are able to pass particularly offensive legislation in the dead of night when the majority of their constituents are fast asleep, only to wake up and realize they've been stripped of their rights as they slumbered. And because legislators work only part time, they receive a measly stipend that is impossible to live on unless they live in a two-income household, are independently wealthy, or have a job that lets them take off six full months every couple of years. This means that none of the folks who can afford to be legislators in Texas come from communities that need representation the most—teachers, laborers, anyone who needs to work full time to survive. The system keeps the voice of the public out by design.

Despite these structural shortcomings, by the beginning of Texas's eighty-fifth legislative session in 2017, the media had elevated the discussion of sexual assault to a pitch that even state Republicans couldn't ignore. Just a few months before, Gretchen Carlson had filed a sexual harassment suit against Fox News head Roger Ailes, threatening the credibility of some voters' main source of information. Furthermore, the month that session kicked off, a federal lawsuit was filed claiming that thirty-one football players at Baylor University—a cultural institution in the Lone Star State that churns out many of its senators and representatives— had committed fifty-two acts of rape from 2011 to 2014. The GOP can and usually does discredit cultural issues prioritized by the "liberal media," but when they came for Fox News and football, the pitchforks hit dangerously close to home.

With millions marching against the party's president, conservative media moguls resigning in light of embarrassing allegations, and now the beloved Baylor boys taking heat, the 2017 legislative session was an opportunity for the GOP to engage in some much-needed damage control. So when we brought our freshly trained and fired-up student advocates into the halls of power to share stories of assault and harassment en masse, we were pleasantly surprised to see Republican legislators at least pretending to listen. And when our girls helped draft and propose a slew of some fifteen bills that would attack the issue from a variety of angles—from building a system for electronic rape kit tracking to funding sexual assault nurse examiners—some of these legislators even reached across the aisle to work with us.

They would go only so far in their support of our work; for example, bills we pushed to better define the nature of consent for the purposes of prosecuting sexual assault cases were a no-go. But ultimately we were able to pass seven laws over the course of six months, leaving Texas—a state that rarely comes in first when it comes to positive human rights metrics—with the most comprehensive sexual assault protections in the country.

Many of these laws would directly benefit our students, such as the Good Samaritan Law, which said that college students who report a sexual assault would not be punished for violating the university's code of conduct (i.e., underage students who were drinking when they witnessed or experienced a sexual assault wouldn't face repercussions for reporting the incident). All of these laws were driven by our students, whether they wrote them directly—in conjunction with legislative aides—or assiduously tracked and advocated for them over the course of their spring semester. They headed off to their summer holidays beaming with pride; Wendy and I heaved a collective sigh of relief and exhaustion.

Session and the school year had ended. The natural break in our programming meant it was time for us to shift into fundraising mode to ensure we could replicate our work for many legislative sessions to come. This entailed less time in the capital city and more in the office, where one day I took a break from emails to flip through a copy of *Vogue* magazine. In it was an article about a Belgian model, Hanne Gaby Odiele, who had just publicly come out to the fashion world as an intersex person. Keep in mind, I had never heard this word before; I had been told my whole life that I had a disorder called complete androgen insensitivity syndrome and was being "fixed" but should refrain from talking about it—never that I was born part of a global community of people like me whom I could connect with. But as I was reading Hanne's story—the surgeries, the hormones, being told to keep everything a secret—I started sweating. *Was I intersex?!*

I wanted to know more, but all of a sudden the (empty) office seemed too public and exposed. I drove home, hopped on my computer, and went down a multihour-long rabbit hole deep into the footnotes of Wikipedia. I came to a few startling realizations at age twenty-seven: First, I was, in fact, intersex. Second, there was a whole movement of intersex people looking to fight stigma surrounding our existence and shame in our upbringing. Third, these people were numerous enough to have made it into a mainstream fashion magazine—meaning I surely had met some others in my life and could meet others if I wanted to. In the wee hours of the morning, head spinning, I shut my laptop. I popped a melatonin and tried to sleep but was overwhelmed.

Having realized for the first time I wasn't alone, I suddenly felt even more so . . . I felt the need to share this information with someone but wasn't yet sure who or how. I did know that if Hanne hadn't shared their story, I never would have found this information about myself—information that seemed pretty pivotal in understanding who I was as a human being. I didn't know the way forward, but I did know that I hoped to one day be as brave as Hanne and be able to show up as my full self in the world too. If I could manage to do that, maybe someone else wouldn't go as long as I had feeling completely isolated, always hidden in plain sight.

I didn't have much time to sit with everything I'd just learned, let alone process this barrage of self-recognition, as Wendy and I were set to hit the road soon after. She'd received an invitation for a paid gig from BBYO (B'nai B'rith Youth Organization)—a Jewish teen movement-building organization—to speak at its annual leadership development summit. The summit had been hosted at Perlman Camp, in rural Lake Como, Pennsylvania, since 1959, the year my mom was born. BBYO requested that Wendy visit camp to train their youth leaders from around the world on how to raise their voices and make change—similar to the workshops we led year-round with our Texas students, but on a much larger scale.

"If I'm going to make the trek to the middle-of-nowhere PA," Wendy had briefed me, pushing a stray piece of her ever-perfect blowout behind her ear, "then you're definitely coming with me."

"You know I'm always down for a trip to bumblefuck!" I'd replied, already scanning the internet for hiking trails nearby.

It seemed serendipitously fitting that right after I received this new knowledge about my own identity, we'd be traveling back to the state in which I was raised. In multiple ways, I felt like I was on the precipice of a pilgrimage home. Unaware of the enormity of what her travel companion beside her was wrestling with, Wendy boarded a plane with me to cross the country. We then rented a car and drove deep into the backwoods of my home state to lead a training for hundreds of rising young leaders from around the world.

After the training, we traversed the Catskill Mountains to the Hancock House Hotel—a run-down but historic hotel situated in a New York hamlet just across the state border from Perlman Camp. Arriving at my room, I flopped onto my bed and heaved a sigh, heavy with the whole upheaval of the who-I-knew-myself-to-be thing. Struck by the paradoxes of our situation, and still reeling from the recent yet momentous intersex bomb, I dropped the following rather grandiose caption on an Instagram post:

@WendyDavisTexas and I embarked on quite a trek to the middle of nowhere, but also somewhere special. This region, about equidistant between where I grew up and where I went to college, is truly a land of borders: New York (Hancock) and PA (Lake Como); non-voting, conservative hunters and socially liberal Jewish campers; aging, small-town residents who told us they'd never been on a plane and the next generation of world leaders who'd traveled from Turkey, Argentina, Ukraine and more; relics of an American past and bastions of the global future. We broke bread with some and shared drinks with others and trained a good number but learned more than we taught, from folks on both sides of the spectrum. Maybe if we spend more time sharing stories and listening to one another than defending our borders—geographic and ideological—we'll realize that, though the plot details differ, the trajectories are largely the same. And the borders we draw are, really, just lines in the sand. [IYKYK: The triviality of borders reference was as much about my own intersex body as it was about electoral politics...]

As I pressed "send" on the post, I heard Wendy knocking insistently on the door to my room. "If we're stuck here for the night, we might as well have a couple drinks downstairs," she said, so we descended to Honest Eddie's Tap Room, a wood-paneled tavern on the hotel's ground floor, and slid into a booth. "Let's start with a bottle of merlot and some burgers," she told the waiter before turning to me and slumping into the cushioned seat. "So many kids in one room for so many hours. Today was awesome but really took it out of me!"

I'm not sure whether it was the wine or the hotel's progressive history—FDR once spoke from the balcony when he was governor of New York—or the brave stories the campers had shared with us, or the fact that I'd just written what I hoped was a poignant post about how borders are bullshit (most likely it was the copious amounts of wine we'd delved into), but sitting across from my hero who'd since become like another mother to me, miles away from the trappings of our lives and anyone we knew, I felt a surge of vulnerability: "Wendy, I'd like to tell you something before we head back to Texas, in case you want to fire me and look for a replacement."

Her eyes widened with concern as she took another sip; who knows what she was expecting to come out of my mouth. I continued, "So you know how you sometimes read *Vogue* magazine?—because you're so fashionable and all," I started, attempting to butter her up with a compliment before I dropped a bomb that I was sure would be grounds for my termination. She nodded, looking more confused than ever, as I forged forward: "Well, I was flipping through a copy in the office and there was a story in it about a model named Hanne Gaby Odiele. Hanne is something called intersex. Do you know what that means?"

This time she shook her head, still unblinking.

"I didn't either before reading the article." I took another gulp of red, spilling a bit on the table. "But it basically means that some people are born biologically between male and female, like with certain parts that don't match what you'd expect just by looking at them—and in the article she talked about these surgeries that were forced onto her as a kid and hormones she has to take because of that and how doctors told her to never tell anyone and how she was always afraid when she was dating that someone would find out. And, well, I'd never heard that word before—they always just told me I have complete androgen insensitivity syndrome—but her story sounded just like mine, so that night I went down a Wikipedia rabbit hole for like six hours and as it turns out, I'm intersex too." Then I downed the rest of my glass.

Wendy paused for a moment, her initial concern softening from apprehension to something more caring. "I'm honored that you're telling me this, truly," she said, "but I'm waiting for the part that explains why I'm supposed to fire you."

I took a deep breath. "Oh, well, you know, we do so much advocacy for abortion rights and I can never get pregnant, so I just figured perhaps you'll be upset that I wasn't truthful with you and maybe you'll want to hire someone in my place who actually has experienced an abortion or might one day." I sloshed another deep pour from the bottle into my glass. "I'm just so inspired by all of our students' vulnerability, sharing what they've been through in a way that they might heal themselves and help others, but I've felt like such a hypocrite the whole time... this is such a big piece of who I am and has colored more parts of my lived experience than you can imagine and it's gotten to the point where I can't keep it bottled in anymore."

This time Wendy grabbed the bottle, emptying it into her own glass as I rambled on.

"So I've realized that as much as our work means to me, my story needs to be told and I want to share it in a way that might make some real change for people like me—just like our girls do. They're honestly the teachers here; I've learned so much from their bravery and from yours. So if my 'coming out' is going to cause issues for us as an organization, I totally understand. I just can't stay trapped in the closet... I've been in here twenty-seven years too long. And I hope that if I break free it will give more people the opportunity to do the same, like reading Hanne's story did for me." I averted my gaze into the glass of wine I was gripping with both hands like a life raft. Then Wendy reached across the table and squeezed my hands with her own.

"First off, I am so very proud of you," Wendy said. "Both for helping me build and run this organization but also for living out Deeds' mission in the most beautiful way I could imagine." I inhaled, realizing I'd been holding my breath for who knows how long. "This is exactly what we want for our girls *and* what I want for you—to be free from the shame society places on women's bodies that weighs on us our entire lives. Your burden is a bit different and yet very much the same." I raised my eyes to meet her gaze as she continued: "This must all seem so scary and overwhelming, but if I can relieve at least one fear for you—I absolutely will not be firing you for being born the way you are. The fact that you still advocate so passionately for a woman's right to choose, even though you'll never face that same decision, only demonstrates what a beautiful human you are and how valuable you are to this movement."

I exhaled.

"Can you imagine if men took up the cause, as you have, how much farther along in the work we'd be? Regardless of what anatomy you were born with, you have a place here at Deeds Not Words and I'm honored to have you on our team—today of all days."

Wendy's acceptance was validating in so many ways. That I thought she'd fire me for being intersex is a legitimate fear—many folks in the South are let go, or not hired in the first place, on the basis of their discrepancy from gender norms—but it was emblematic of a larger psychological struggle. When doctors and family members tell you as a kid to never share who you really are because you'll be ridiculed by peers and will struggle to find a partner when you're older, you internalize that to mean *I am inherently unworthy of love and acceptance, simply for existing.* Believing that Wendy would boot me because I could never have an abortion, therefore shouldn't be a face of abortion-forward work, was an adult permutation of the lack of belonging I've felt in every space I've occupied as long as I can remember.

I've never felt like I truly fit in anywhere. The tough part of being an intersex woman is you're too this or not enough that. I don't fully identify with cisgender women because I don't get a period, can't get pregnant, and have had very different life experiences as an intersex person. At the same time, being femme and able to "pass" as cisgender, I've experienced so much traditional misogyny that many less-binary-appearing intersex folks haven't. And because I look the way I do, with both its attendant privilege and its misconceptions, I often feel "not intersex enough" to fit into the intersex spaces that are heavily queer and visibly nonbinary—like I don't belong even in the place for people who don't belong. I know this is an ongoing form of my inner child's struggle with truly believing that I'm welcome and wanted, wherever I am. But coming out to Wendy was the first step in a shift in my thinking. It was my first time reaching out for a life preserver in a sea I wasn't sure I was supposed to swim in, and she didn't let me drown.

Wendy serving as that bridge over troubled water (please excuse the corny metaphor) helped me realize that I also could be a bridge. Besides being a literal bridge between the male and female sexes, I started to understand that bridging communities has permeated other areas of my life as well. I am often a bridge between my conservative family members and my leftist advocate comrades. Growing up, I bridged my middle-class immediate family with the extremely wealthy folks I went to school with and my after-school co-workers—who came from Philadelphia proper, or less wealthy suburbs, to work where I lived to get better tips. As Wendy and I packed our things to head back from the state where I grew up to the one I now call home, I pondered how I might continue to serve in this role in other spaces that desperately needed to bridge a chasm of understanding. Little did I know, the Texas State Legislature would provide me such an opportunity (bless their heart) so soon after arriving back in the Lone Star State...

ELLIPSIS . . .

An ellipsis symbolizes omission; something has been left out.
But it also signifies continuation—the journey isn't done yet . . .

Sometimes the meaning or significance of something hits you only in hindsight, though it's something the universe knew all along. I got a tattoo of three dots—an ellipsis—on Friday the thirteenth, a day when tattoo parlors traditionally offer cheap prices for a set short list of easy designs. I didn't know at the time that this tattoo sometimes symbolizes "a slow change of idea or thought," which is basically what I've devoted my entire life to as an activist. And apparently the ellipsis tattoo most frequently intends to raise awareness of mental health struggles but also connotes hope: life goes on and there are still more good things to come. Striving for mental wellness has been a huge component of my experience as an intersex person and as someone with bipolar disorder—another heavily stigmatized and shame-ridden facet of my identity, which we'll delve into later.

The word "ellipsis" itself, though, "comes from the Greek word meaning 'omission,' and that's just what it does: an ellipsis shows that something has been left out" (www.grammarly.com). As I'd expressed to Wendy back in PA, we urged our student advocates to own the struggles and share them so that they might feel less alone and welcome others into understanding their journey—but there was a huge piece of my own journey that I'd left out of all of my advocacy. This glaring omission from my work was weighing on me, and I decided that it was time to fill in some of the gaps pertaining to who I really was for people in my life, both personally and professionally. I also wanted to fill in some gaps in my own life (pun intended); having been glued to Wendy and our students for the previous six months, I didn't have much of a sex life to speak of and decided it was high time for a hot girl summer.

That said, dating pretty much sucks. I don't know how some people profess to like it . . . I hear they're into, you know, getting dressed up and the excitement of meeting someone new and getting their meal paid for. I probably just remember this concept from rom coms, because I don't know many women who actually *do* like dating, except maybe my single mom friends who are so overjoyed for an excuse to get out of the house for an evening that they'll put up with small talk from any rando—or worse, listen to a rando drone on, nonstop, for hours without asking one question about their life in return. Dating is dedicating precious hours of

your life to someone you're not even sure you'll like and probably won't ever see again, when you could have been cuddling your
pup or dancing with your friends or going to sleep at 9:30 p.m.
and getting a full nine hours. All for the slim chance that maybe
this will be your person, for a lifetime or maybe a few bone sessions. It has never been on my top ten list of favorite activities.

I was on a mission, though, to get some. It was time to start
putting myself out there again. My first date back on the wagon
ended up being one of those nights when I had one–or two,
probably three–too many drinks to stave off the boredom of
yet another dude who isn't aware that a conversation involves
asking questions and showing reciprocal interest in what the
other person has to say. And it's too bad for them because I like
to talk about some really enthralling shit–whether it be that time
I talked my way out of a bribe near the Mozambican border with
a can of Pringles, or my favorite pastime of watching Kardashian
reruns while texting my neighbor about whether it might be
time for me to start getting Chiquita's anal glands expressed.
(That's Chihuahua healthcare, by the way, not some new kink.)

That night was no great story to share on another future
date. I don't even remember his name or where we went before
I arrived home, drunk at 10 p.m., realizing I really could have cut
the whole thing short and been under the covers by 9:30 after all.
Then it hit me . . . that guy hadn't asked me one question about
myself, I hadn't gotten to share any of my stories, but there was
someone I *could* share stories with who *had* to listen–at least for
two minutes of allotted time: Lois Kolkhorst, Texas state senator
and all around terrible human being.

I had seen Lois a lot recently. Besides Deeds' sexual assault legislation, we'd just spent the entire six-month legislative session at the Capitol fighting the infamous "bathroom bill," which would require trans folks to pee in the bathroom that aligns with the original sex on their birth certificate. (Which isn't even enforceable, by the way... who carries their birth certificate around with them?!) Although a huge coalition of individuals was against it—activists and business owners and basically anyone who realizes that we should probably be focusing on something more important than where, how, or when anyone pees—Lois wasn't having any of it. She and her cronies Lieutenant Governor Dan Patrick and some others wouldn't let this thing die. When the bill actually did die, that is, consistently was voted down and ultimately failed, they were so butthurt about it that they decided to call ANOTHER "special session" of the legislature. This meant bringing all the senators and representatives back from around the state for an extra month—using our hard-earned taxpayer dollars to do so—just to try to pass this one bathroom bill again. It's honestly ludicrous, but also just another day in Texas politics.

The morning of that lame, booze-soaked date, Wendy and I had given yet another advocacy training. This time, we included a broader swath of activists beyond our students—given that we'd need a much larger show of opposition to effectively end an anti-LGBTQIA+ initiative in the South, where they tend to succeed—but it was all still feeling pretty déjà vu. Then I met Danielle Skidmore. Danielle happens to be trans, so she has XY chromosomes like I do—not that she, or anyone, knew that about me at the time. She is also from Philadelphia so we ended up reminiscing about our hometown, which felt safe and comforting in the midst of an attack on our basic human rights. She told me she frequently came to the Capitol to advocate against this kind of lunacy, so we ended up exchanging social media follows before going about our days—unaware that later that same evening, this budding friendship would be taken to a whole 'nother level (pretty sure that's Philly jargon right there).

Fast-forward twelve hours and I was drunkenly logged into Facebook chat, seeing who was still up that I could run my new idea past—someone who'd get it. In a stroke of fate, one of the few people online at that hour was Danielle. Yes, I'd literally only met her once, for about five minutes, and messaging her late at night was thoroughly strange and borderline creepy. But she's openly trans, which means she knew how to come out—something I had attempted, when drunk, only with Wendy and had no idea how to navigate publicly. If I was going to share my story—this particular story—with Lois Kolkhorst, I needed help in figuring out how to divulge it. Because although I was used to sharing personal stories at least ten times a week in committee hearings or on the Senate floor, this one was different.

The story of my lived experience as an intersex person was lodged so deep in my soul that only way too much alcohol could lubricate the hinges enough to open the door of its prison a smidge. This time, that door was cracked far enough open—or maybe I was just generally pissed off enough, after having spent seven damn months talking about this stupid bathroom bill, or both—that I decided it was time to finally set this story free. Plus, Lois Kolkhorst kept talking about how "biological sex is cut and dried" and once we went back to enforcing that clear distinction all these trans perverts would go back where they came from. But biological sex is not cut and dried; around 2 percent of humans, something like 160 million people, are born somewhere in between like me.

Yes, I have a vagina, like the people Lois wanted tinkling in the ladies' room. But I was also born with internal testes, before the doctors took them from me. A group of people roughly half the size of the US population are born with traits that don't fit neatly into an "M" or "F" category. If bigots like Lois wanted to pass discriminatory legislation, they should at least open a biology textbook first. But science isn't a strong suit of Texas legislators; I guess it was up to me to teach them.

When you're drunk, as I was at that point, you pee more frequently than usual. So when I took my perhaps fourth trip to the bathroom since arriving home, I started thinking: if my sex, based on my anatomy, wasn't neatly represented by either of those stick figure emblems on the doors of public restrooms, then where was I supposed to pee . . . outside? I'd get arrested for public urination! Is that what Lois wanted? That seemed pretty messy, not to mention unsanitary, and probably was not the best use of law enforcement's time. It was about time that I raised these vital questions—in the morning, after I sobered up—because I figured they'd clear things up for everyone: Lois and her boys would realize that the premise of the bathroom bill was inherently flawed, people like Danielle could pee in peace, and everyone could just go home.

With the urgency of this information, and of somehow more

urine in my bladder, I initiated that fateful Facebook chat with Danielle.

Hi, Danielle! Nice meeting you today. Do you have a second?
I know it's late.

Sure.

I think I want to testify against the Bathroom Bill
tomorrow ...

I assumed as much—you were leading a whole training
on it earlier this morning ...

(As I learned later, in her head she was thinking something more like, "Sure, cis straight white girl—we need all the allies we can get." But I was about to burst that bubble ...)

Right, but I think I want to testify against it as an intersex
person.

Oh, wow. OK—let's chat.

At that point, Danielle and I discussed the nuances of coming out as someone who doesn't fit into the confines of the traditional paradigms of gender and sex:

Have you come out to your friends and family?

No.

OK. Do you feel ready to do this?

Not really.

I don't think I'd actually fully considered the implications of what I was about to do—that coming out in front of a body of elected officials meant that I'd also then be "out" in all other contexts. But the sheer nonsensicality and cruelty of this proposed legislation necessitated bold action, in my mind, and the rest of these considerations could be earmarked for some future date following the death of the bill.

After Danielle walked me through what coming out was like, a conversation that left me only more riled up by nerves and conviction in the importance of what I wanted to do, I realized that I should probably notify a few people besides Danielle. First and foremost, my actions reflected the organization that employed me and my boss, who happened to be a former colleague of Lois and the lot. Wendy was no stranger to pulling stunts to make "good trouble," like when she filibustered for those thirteen hours straight. That action was the stuff of feminist legend and the whole reason I relocated to the Lone Star State to work for her in the first place. If anyone knew how to make a statement to kill a bill, it was Wendy. So although it was well after midnight at that point, I decided the moment was desperate enough that I could disrupt her slumber with a phone call for some much-needed guidance.

I think Wendy had, coincidentally, just woken up to use the

restroom (*cosmic alignment*) so she actually picked up my 3 a.m. phone call. My prior sloshy buzz having given way to anxiety-ridden anticipation of what was about to go down the next morning, I gave her a frantic CliffsNotes version of my conversation with Danielle and what I'd decided to do. Wendy loved it. She was proud of me for deciding to embody the spirit of Deeds Not Words, taking courageous action to heal myself and protect others. She ended the call with one main suggestion: "I think you should try to look as feminine as possible when you walk into that committee room. I know you don't wear makeup, but maybe throw on a bit of lipstick, a killer dress, and some power heels." Wendy often advises that heels bring confidence, adding a little height and some power to your posture. "That way when you take the dais, all those old legislators' minds will be wandering—we know some of them have even tried to hit on you before—and it will really throw them for a loop when you drop the fact that you were, you know, born with balls." The woman sure knows how to make an entrance!

After hanging up with Wendy, I started readying myself for the morning's shenanigans. I selected a yellow dress from my closet splashed with purpley pink flowers, not even aware at the time that the intersex flag is yellow and purple or that orchids symbolize our community (more cosmic alignment!). Pulling a tube of mascara from the cabinet behind my mirror, I caught a glimpse of my face; it didn't look quite as confident as I'd hoped—as someone who was about to pull something like this off was supposed to look. The clock on my phone showed 3:58 a.m., and all of a sudden I felt completely alone. So I did what any internet-addled former nineties kid would do and went back online for reinforcements.

Strangely enough, Mia—then UT student, badass sexual assault advocate, and one of my favorite Deeds Not Words mentees—was on Facebook chat . . . and this was when the student became the teacher.

I confirmed that Mia was indeed up and hadn't just left her computer open. Miraculously, she responded right away. I asked whether she could read my drafted testimony and edit it for me, since this was the first time I was going public with certain info—a role reversal from our usual exchanges, when I'd give her feedback on her speeches. She agreed and then responded:

> *Alicia, this is so powerful. Amazing. I wouldn't change*
> *one word.*

Thanks! I feel good about it and it feels like the right
time but I wanted to review it with someone who is good
at this stuff, and equally powerful.

> *I think it's awesome. I'd never thought of these issues in*
> *this context before and it's incredibly striking.*

Yeah, what [trailblazer State Rep.] Senfronia Thompson said
in the regular session is true. Whether about Black folks in
the "separate but equal" era or trans folks now, it was never
about bathrooms—it was always about discrimination.

> *You're going to kill it! I'm definitely going to try to go to register*
> *my position. I don't have anything from personal experience to*

> *say on tomorrow's bills, and I think that space should be taken*
> *up by people who do, but I want to be there in solidarity.*

What if I picked you up to bring you? . . . at 6:30 AM?
Because there will be so many speakers, I want to be one
of the first to register.

> *That would actually be awesome! I'll probably just*
> *watch Game of Thrones till then.*

I coordinated the necessary logistical details, took a deep breath, and started applying eyeliner. Knowing I wouldn't be alone, I started to see this act of courage more clearly. After finishing my makeup and choking down coffee (like my hands weren't shaking enough already), I hopped in my car just as the sun was starting to rise. As I plugged Mia's address into Google Maps, I realized I had one more person to call. My mother lives on the East Coast, so it was just about when she'd be getting up to make her own coffee.

"Mom, I'm doing it today," I told her. "I'm en route to the Capitol now and I'm going to share my story."

"Are you sure you want to do this? Have you thought through all the implications?"

"Probably not," I admitted, "but it finally feels right."

At that point, I had expected way more pushback. My family had kept this secret so tightly bottled for twenty-seven years, and I don't think my parents had ever expected to take the lid off. But my mom seemed fine with it.

"Okay. I love you," she said. "Let me know how it goes."

Mia and I parked and walked up to the big pink marble building where so many big, hard, and lasting decisions are made. It looked extra pink in the morning light—such a benign, almost friendly color that feels incongruous if you know what happens within. The committee rooms for these sort of hearings are located deep in the bowels of the building. We took the elevator down into the depths and found an already lengthy line of people who wanted to register to speak. What happened after that is pretty blurry. Luckily, because I don't remember much, my remarks were printed out and caught on camera. But I do recall catching sight of Danielle before entering the hearing and greeting her:

You're here!
You think I'd let you do this alone?

A few hours after arriving at the Capitol, many hours after I'd last slept, I stepped into that basement room. I crossed in front of a raised platform of stoic senators—determined to appear raptly concerned when a Republican took the lectern (the vast minority of public attendees for this particular hearing) and entirely uninterested when a speaker poked holes in the bill. Mia and I took seats in the audience to wait our turn and snapped a few selfies for good measure. When they called my name, I took the podium and apparently delivered some iteration of the following predrafted testimony—the biggest moment of my life truncated by their uncaring "time's up" buzzer:

Madam Chairperson and Members of the Committee,

My name is Alicia Roth Weigel, I am a resident of Austin, the director of a gender equality nonprofit, and I have XY chromosomes. I stand here today representing the "I" in LGBTQIA in the hopes that, because I look more gender-"normal" in the current societal conception of what that means, you might hear my words in a different light. Any discrimination stems from a lack of understanding, after all.

"I" stands for intersex. Because of a condition called complete androgen insensitivity, I was born phenotypically female, with a "woman's" anatomy on the outside, but internal testes instead of ovaries—that were subsequently removed as to not become "precancerous." This practice is now heavily contested only twenty-seven years later, in light of the exponential advancement of modern medicine, as it is a remnant of this still present gender "ideal," and wanting to "normalize" children from birth to avoid a life of hardship and shame.

While I find it absurd that I have to disclose my anatomical history to a room of complete strangers, legislators no less, that makes me feel more compelled to do so. Because while I'll unfortunately never bear children, I am extremely privileged to have been born in a way that my discrepancy from the gender "norm" is not immediately apparent—not worn on my sleeve—and that has saved me much persecution up to this point.

I can tell you that I am very much a woman. Not that every woman—or any race, or any group of people—has any particular tendency, I paint my toenails, I read US Weekly.

My mom will tell you I refused to wear pants as a kid, insisting on only purple or pink skirts, and I had way too many Barbies. I help manage Wendy Davis's nonprofit focused on women's rights because my experiences as a victim of discrimination in the workplace, a survivor of sexual assault, and so much more bind me to the common plight of what it means to be a woman.

Does that mean that, because of my genotypic XY chromosomes, I've been using the wrong bathroom my whole life? No. It means who cares what bathroom I use? If my life experience is equal to that of a female, I should be able to identify as such. And I do...

I am a woman. And regardless of my gender, a bathroom is a bathroom. It's a place where all humans, regardless of gender, engage in a common activity we unfortunately have not yet evolved out of.

I urge you to reconsider your feelings on what I feel is an extremely harmful piece of legislation—one that tying your name to will, I believe, tarnish your legacy as a legislator, as generations become more accepting of, and adamant about enforcing, civil rights. If not for the betterment of the lives of others you don't know and may never understand, think of your own families and how you want them to appear in history books. Please vote no on Senate Bill 3.

The senators asked me no questions; based on the glaring flaws of this particular piece of legislation, it was in their best interest not to do so. But this two-minute testimony unearthed a lifetime of questions elsewhere. These started with the reporters who flanked me as I left the room; fellow activists who texted, having followed coverage from home; and sympathetic state legislators who caught me in the hall after rushing away from the little TVs in their offices. I felt dizzy, almost drunk like the night before. Sharing your biggest secret in front of a room full of strangers on too little sleep and too much caffeine will do that to you. But it was also a happy dizzy.

I didn't have any answers to anyone's questions yet, let alone my own. I honestly felt more confused about the way forward than I had the day before and more vulnerable than I thought was possible, but I also felt free. This was the great story I'd get to share on future dates, once I felt comfortable doing so (which would take years). With the death of the bathroom bill, I was reborn. And after all that coffee, I honestly really had to pee, so I made my way to the right restroom for me.

I had now started to fill in the space an ellipsis had held in my life for so long, but this was just the first step. I was "out" to the Texas Senate but not yet to my friends and family. And given that the vast majority of the world had no idea what intersex means, coming out is unfortunately a daily reality—whether to access the care I need in an insufficiently trained doctor's office or because a business associate has Googled my name and has questions. But I had entered into a new phase of reality, for sure. The ellipsis had been a place-filler for the hole in my story. Now it signified that the work wasn't done yet and was, in fact, just beginning. Many folks get an ellipsis tattoo as a symbol of progress, or a journey that ultimately takes the individual somewhere different in their lives, for better or worse, and that's exactly what I was about to embark on. The chapter of my life in the closet was ending. And in many ways, at twenty-seven years old, my life was just beginning.

I EXYST

I am a woman and I have XY chromosomes. We exist; I ExyST.

IEXYST

One thing I can guarantee about ex(y)sting in public as an intersex person is you won't be alone for long. A few quick internet searches and perusing social media will quickly gain you access to a worldwide network of intersex individuals, clustered around a variety of organizations that create online and in-person forums for building community. Given that thousands of Texans had registered to testify against the bathroom bill and had come from all across the state to do so, I didn't even have to hop on a computer before finding others; Houston-based activists Mo Cortez and Koomah had found and approached me minutes after seeing my testimony on one of the television screens distributed throughout the Capitol.

I'll be honest, I kind of came out backwards—sharing my identity with a host of legislators and crowds of strangers before even notifying my own brother. So when Mo and Koomah congratulated me, I probably wasn't quite ready yet to be welcomed into that community. I took note of their names, but with a vulnerability hangover setting in, I wanted nothing more than to return home to some semblance of familiarity. After quickly sharing my contact info with a representative from GLAAD (Gay and Lesbian Alliance Against Defamation) who was interested in sharing what had happened with their national network of reporters, I booked it out of the Capitol to the safety of my car. As I was driving home, what I'd just done began to set in.

First off, I'd divulged some information about my genitals and reproductive anatomy in a way that I, and most other people, are unaccustomed to doing outside of a doctor's office. Second, I had no idea how everyone in my life would react to the news that I'd lied to them my whole life, was not who they thought I was, and was a member of a community they'd probably only heard about as the butt of a joke. I knew that if I were them, I might feel slighted if I found out online before hearing from me; I also knew that I was exhausted from not sleeping the night before and reclaiming my identity for the first time in the context of a public spectacle. I didn't have it in me to call each and every person who meant something to me in order to tell them so I decided that pulling the video footage of my testimony from records available online and texting it to 90 percent of the contacts in my phone was a good place to start.

The one phone call I did make was to a family member who

I knew was intersex too. This person is much older than me–from a generation where acceptance of difference was far less common than it is now and medical practice was way more primordial–so although we both knew we had this human condition in common, we'd actually never spoken about it. This person was taught, as I had been, that we were a defective [insert "male" or "female" sex] rather than a human being who simply broke the mold. I had credited this to a generational difference, but in fact so many intersex people today are still inculcated into this mindset and continue to uphold this view.

Another family member one generation elder even to this particular relative took their own life, after never having children and contracting a mysterious cancer; so much of me wonders if they were intersex too and if we could have broken beyond the barriers of silence that keep us lonely, perhaps things might have turned out differently. The stigma surrounding our identity prevents us from truly knowing even our own family members; in doing so, it detracts from our ability to truly know ourselves too. If this past paragraph seems confusing: welcome to the club. When your existence is shrouded in secrecy, the roots of your family tree get lost in cobwebs…

Out of respect for my relative's privacy, I won't divulge the details of the phone conversation they and I had that day I came out. I will confirm it was brief, confusing, and awkward; in the five years I've now been out, it has been repeated only once since and without much more success. In the five short minutes it took to complete that call, though, I'd received about a hundred others. Since I lacked the energy and desire to speak to anyone else at that point, these unanswered calls gave way to more text messages than I could open or respond to.

The cool thing is, I'm lucky enough to be surrounded by open-minded individuals who care more about me than they do about clinging to outdated or discriminatory ideals; the response was overwhelmingly positive and supportive. But overwhelmed was the overarching feeling I could identify at the time—above pride, fear, or any other emotional reaction to the events of the day. I decided to seclude myself for the weekend, to give myself a chance to process. As I do to this day, I turned to nature: I spent Saturday reading Gabriel García Márquez's *One Hundred Years of Solitude* (fitting how I now looked back on my life before coming out) on a swing under the great live oak trees at the Lady Bird Johnson Wildflower Center and Sunday swimming solo at McKinney Falls State Park.

By Monday, I hadn't yet mustered the courage to read, let alone respond to, all the texts that continued to flood in. I did feel ready to break my solitude but only with someone who might understand something similar to what I was going through. I first went online and reached out to as many intersex activists as I could find via Instagram direct messages, including the organization interACT, which I'd gathered was some sort of central clearinghouse for the community in the United States. Then I picked up the phone and gave Danielle Skidmore a call:

Hey Danielle. How are you feeling after the bill passed out of the Senate?

Hi there. We'll show back up and make sure it doesn't continue on past the House later this month. But how are YOU feeling after Friday?

I'm not sure I know how to answer that question on a personal level yet. I've managed to text my brother back and a couple other close friends—everyone's been super accepting, which makes me super lucky in comparison to what you and so many others have had to go through . . .

That doesn't make it easy, though; give yourself time.

I feel like I need to respond to everyone who's shown support, but it just seems so daunting to have a million different conversations and try to respond to questions I'm not even sure I know how to answer yet.

Why don't you write a post that you can share on social media, outlining what you know and don't know, how you feel and what you're not ready to share yet . . . Level-set with folks so that you buy yourself some time to figure this all out for yourself, before having to answer to the rest of the world.

Not a bad idea—lemme go do that now.

I took to our organizational Medium page, encapsulating the previous seventy-two hours from the vantage point of my work with Deeds Not Words; even if I didn't have the personal part down yet and was still struggling to understand what I was feeling, a professional lens was helpful at least to organize my thoughts. I penned a piece titled "Putting the 'I' in LGBTQIA+," anchored on

Wendy's favorite quote from the former presidential spouse who gave the Lady Bird Johnson Wildflower Center its name: "Become so wrapped up in something that you forget to be afraid." That was exactly how I felt. I'd been blinded to the fear, confusion, everything that was now setting in, just a few days before—so convinced that this bathroom bill was a terrible idea for so many— that I hadn't registered potential consequences for myself:

> *When I realized how much was at stake, should this piece of legislation pass—60,000 jobs, 600,000 already extremely vulnerable people's sense of safety in their everyday lives—I couldn't not say something. Based on my own birth certificate (which reads "female" rather than "intersex," as it does for many with related "conditions"), this bill would not affect me personally. But keeping my story to myself became privilege when my withholding it left others in harm's way.*

The piece was shared far and wide, from old friends in Brazil on Facebook to old business colleagues from my tech days on LinkedIn. I realized that the can of worms I'd opened couldn't be shut and I needed to keep spilling it but would need more time to do so. Deeds Not Words wasn't about me; it was about the kids we worked with. I needed space to be able to figure out my own path forward, and I wasn't going to get it while helping train hundreds of young women a year to step foot onto their own.

I was gaining my own platform, separate from Wendy's that I'd originally hopped onto—invited to speak at the worldwide South by Southwest (SXSW) conference and being featured in media from Refinery29 to BuzzFeed News. I needed to figure out how to wield that and what to do with it. Plus, given that half of the world's population are women, I justified that Wendy would have ample options to replace me. Meeting at SXSW fellow intersex activists Emily Quinn and Jahni Leggett—who'd been out longer and had a better sense of the broader movement than I did at that point—confirmed for me that there were far fewer out intersex activists than women's rights activists, far far far fewer. The need for my voice was much greater on *that* stage. It was clear to me that my time at Deeds was drawing to a close, but I did have to figure out how I was going to pay my bills if I left...

As the spotlight on me grew, so it did on Danielle as well. The city of Austin was growing unsustainably, generating a housing crisis similar to San Francisco's and traffic that began to rival Houston's—everyone's worst nightmare. Not only is Danielle a civil engineer, with the skills and vision to help turn our growth trajectory around, but also an out trans woman in Texas. Organizations and press frequently turned to her expertise, both her lived and professional experience, to help navigate an uncertain future for our city and state. I asked her whether she'd ever considered running for office:

People have been urging me to run for quite some time now, and the asks are getting more and more frequent.

So why don't you?

For starters, my son, Peter, is nonverbal and in a wheelchair. Caring for him takes so much of my time and we get very little help; dividing that with my ex—who doesn't get paid as much as she deserves, as a professor—doesn't make that any easier.

I hear you and I can't pretend to imagine what that's like. But what I also hear you saying is that besides being a trans transportation engineer, you can also speak to disability rights and the failures of our current educational system. Sounds like your voice is even more needed and relevant than I originally thought.

I'm also an introvert… and a nerd.

Luckily you have a professional marketer here who can help translate your geek-talk into digestible English and has media-trained countless professionals in public speaking…

So what YOU'RE saying is, if I do this—you would come along for the ride?

An intersex woman running a trans woman's campaign in Texas would be pretty epic. We're striving for something much bigger than a City Council district. Plus, we're two XY bitches from Philly … we understand each other; we'd be partners in this!

Well then giddy up, pardner!

Thus began our campaign to elect the first out trans person to public office in the State of Texas and the first transportation engineer to the Austin City Council.

The only thing was, I had no idea how to run a political campaign. Luckily I had access to one woman who certainly did. I was nervous to tell Wendy that I'd be leaving Deeds to take on this new challenge but also knew that she'd be supportive. She hadn't fired me when I first came out to her, but I think she realized then that my journey might move in a different direction from what we both originally thought it would when I first landed in Texas. When I told her about my potential job pivot, not only was she not angry—she was excited. We made a plan to hire a team to put on the various hats I'd been wearing, as Deeds' model had proved its worth and we'd brought in sufficient funding to grow the organization into its next phase too. Then she helped me understand the basics of what I'd need to plan my next venture into campaign management.

"You know I started out on the City Council in Fort Worth, and that was some of the most meaningful work I've done to date," Wendy reminisced as we discussed my future. "You're so connected to the needs of everyday people and gain so much perspective. Plus, you learn what it looks like to actually implement everything we set in motion by passing the type of legislation we work on at Deeds. I'm grateful for what you've helped build here, and mounting a campaign will be an entirely different learning curve, but I've seen how you figure things out on the fly. We'll miss you, but you'll always be part of the Deeds Not Words family. I'm here to help, and we'll all be here cheering y'all on." With this vote of confidence, Danielle and I took the plunge. I left my job and she left hers in April 2018 to run full speed toward the October election.

From Day 1, the broader reception of our campaign was a lot more mixed than the blessing we'd received from Wendy. We spoke to many Austinites desperate for real change and grateful we were putting ourselves out there to make that happen. But many of those people—even some we counted as close friends—were wary enough of our prospects to avoid publicly voicing that support. We were running against an entrenched incumbent who'd already served two terms on Council, and the political establishment always hesitates to embrace new candidates when the risk is much higher to do so. Plus, our opponent had enough personal wealth to self-fund a large portion of what it would take to stay in power. She had name recognition and the advantage of some hired guns from her prior races, who were well-versed in what it took to win. Meanwhile, I was a novice campaign manager, relying on what I learned in the Campaign School run by Annie's List—an organization that works to elect progressive women in Texas—and a scrappy can-do attitude.

We were buoyed by the fact that the sitting council members had allowed Austin's current pain points to develop and that what Danielle lacked in political know-how, she made up for in engineering experience to fix things. We also felt her story would resonate more with University of Texas students, a sizable constituency in the district we were running for—if we could persuade them to turn out to vote, make it all the way down the ballot to where the local races are printed, and remember Danielle's name. Plus, trans and intersex folks are used to fighting for visibility against all odds; we could use that to our advantage too. We quickly attracted attention on the national stage—from spots on Logo TV to *The Young Turks*—which we used to establish legitimacy and raise funds beyond the confines of Austin's political elite. But the most viral media exposure we garnered turned out to be a lot more complicated . . .

By that point of the campaign, I'd moved out of my rental and back into the supporter housing where I'd lived when I first arrived in Austin. As much as I didn't want to live in that building again, campaign finance law restricts local races to small-dollar donations, meaning we'd be running our entire operation on a shoestring budget. A well-run campaign allocates the majority of its assets to field activities—direct voter contact, door-to-door, and the materials and personnel to support it—not to campaign staff salaries. The opportunity to remove rent from my own cost of living for the duration of our race was too good to pass up, especially in a city where housing is some of the most expensive in the country. Plus, living downtown gave me access to voters who live in high-rises, who are much harder to reach than people in single-family homes when knocking on doors, given the barriers of security guards and elevator codes.

Danielle also lives downtown, at least part time, because her downtown apartment is more accessible for her son than a house with stairs. She and her ex split their time caring for Peter in the apartment and then rotating to stay in their original family home in the nearby neighborhood of Clarksville when they weren't on kid duty—a difficult yet necessary arrangement that perhaps only separated parents of a child with disabilities could make work. We established our official campaign headquarters in the Clarksville house to save additional overhead costs and to ease the burden on Danielle's already extremely complicated schedule. We then worked out of the reservable common areas of her and my downtown residences on the weeks when Peter was in her care. Everyone who followed our campaign closely knew about this living and working arrangement, as it was integral to Danielle's story as a human being trying to exist in systems not built to support those of us who aren't cis and able-bodied. So when my friend Will called one morning and immediately asked whether I was in Clarksville or downtown, I assumed he was trying to stop by the campaign office to pick up campaign literature or something similar.

"If you're downtown, I need you to come down to the corner of Eighth and Congress ASAP," Will demanded. Beyond the urgency in his voice, I registered frustration as he went on: "There's a guy set up outside the Chipotle with a TV crew and a table with a big banner that reads 'There are only two genders. Change my mind.' I feel like you and Danielle are the perfect folks to educate this guy and could maybe spin it into a stunt for the campaign." I hung up and slipped on my shoes.

Heading out the door, I texted Danielle to let her know I was headed to engage with this random guy on a street corner and encouraged her to join me so I could film the interaction and use it in some sort of social media post. When I was less than a block from my building, she'd already texted me back: "Oh girl, I'm already way ahead of you . . ." It turns out that she and Peter had rolled by the table on their morning walk to check our campaign mailbox. My text had reached her when she was already seated and ready to deliver some much-needed education to this ignorant instigator. I picked up my pace.

A more experienced campaign manager would have researched this guy before encouraging her candidate to enter a public debate with him. Had I done that, I would have found out that this asshole on the corner was in fact Steven Crowder, an alt-right pundit who had left Fox News to run a podcast and the YouTube show *Louder with Crowder*, with almost six million subscribers on the video platform alone. I also probably would have recognized that this was the same loser who had dressed in drag, pretended to be trans, and interviewed Wendy while we were at the first Women's March—only to splice what she said to make her look stupid in a video skewering her for his online audience. I definitely would have realized that despite the title of his recurring "Change My Mind" segment, Crowder in fact *never* changes his mind on anything—regardless of the evidence presented to him—instead utilizing this platform to stoke hatred and bigotry among his incel-type followers.

Considering all of this, I probably would have ordered Danielle *not* to engage with him and to continue on her merry way with Peter. But arriving on the scene, I found the two of them already deep in conversation. She had one hand protectively on her son's running stroller and acknowledged me with a quick glance that somehow expressed, all in one look, "You have no idea what you're about to witness," "I'm somewhat amused but also trying to keep myself from mauling this guy," and "Oh, lord— Hurricane Alicia's about to roll through."

I approached the table on the corner where they sat chatting in time to hear Crowder responding to Danielle's factoid of suicide rates among the LGBTQIA+ community: "Suicide rates are actually lower among minorities than they are among white men. Among transgender Americans, the suicide rate is actually higher than it was among slaves or Jews in Auschwitz. Are you telling me that trans folks are treated worse than enslaved Black folks or Jews in the Holocaust?" This was going to be a doozy.

He continued to make assertions about how using proper pronouns divides us more than it connects us ("I've asked folks on the street if they're trans and had them get offended"), how having both a mother and a father was intrinsically better for a household, and more gems that you can feel free to check out online, if you'd like to add yourself to the more than seventeen million views the video currently counts on YouTube. When they finished, I immediately plopped myself down in her vacated seat and introduced myself, cluing Crowder in that I worked for Danielle.

Oh so this is kinda like a double team action?
    That was weird phrasing...

After letting him know Danielle was my boss, I told him I was particularly interested in being part of this conversation on a personal level given that I'm intersex, having been born with body parts from both sides of his binary divide.

If it's irrefutable that 2 percent of the world is born in between, in terms of our biological traits, then how does it not follow that some of us also might identify in between, as far as our gender identity and expression?

He had no answer for me, pivoting to tell me we were there to discuss being transgender, not intersex, and that no one had forced me to sit down and enter this conversation.

There are people like you who don't respect people's identity and basic biology. So no, you didn't force me to sit down, but there are people who are so fed up with having to legitimize our existence on a daily basis when you don't have to do that either . . .

By this point, I was fully riled up. I noticed branded mugs on the table and asked whether he had any water, but he said that would be a liability issue. "We certainly don't want anyone saying I poisoned you," he said. I rolled my eyes and continued my line of thought.

Doctors decide to play God and make a decision on what biological sex a[n intersex] child should have.

Let's remove intersex from the table because we're talking about transgender. These are two different issues, and I'd like to address them separately if I can.

But they're not separate . . . I was assigned "female" by the doctor who worked on me, but I was born in between.

Recognizing that having his viewers internalize what I was saying would be bad for business—his business being the peddling of misinformation—Crowder began to assert that my understanding of the prevalence of intersex people and how our anatomy manifests was flawed.

This pundit is telling me that you know more about the science of my existence than I do. If you want to talk about how our sides can have productive conversations, I think maybe a first step in y'all's camp is not assuming that you know better than everyone else who has lived a certain experience.

I don't, just like I don't interrupt…

Unable to discredit my knowledge, he then pivoted to attack the manner in which I delivered it.

Well I'm sorry, but you're interrupting my day by questioning my existence and my boss's existence.

I haven't questioned your existence, I haven't interrupted you, and I haven't said I know more than you … only you have said that.

Gaslighting at its finest. If you're caught doing something bad, accuse the other party of doing it. He shifted back to how I wasn't even relevant to the conversation because transgenderism is "very different from the genetic anomaly of intersex." I pushed back that gender was also based on something intrinsic that you're born with—like being gay—before we delved into a conversation on the nature of male versus female brains that honestly I shouldn't have touched with a ten-foot pole. Frustrated with the direction this was all headed, I brought us back to the most important question at hand:

If my self does not threaten your daily existence, then why do you care?

It does.

How?

Western Civilization says there is male and female and it is not interchangeable.

So only Western Civilization is right—is that what you're saying?

That's a different conversation, but yes.

Really?!

Yes.

So the whole white supremacist, Western perception of society is what is right?

I don't believe in white supremacy at all.

Well, Western Civilization is arguably founded by the colonization by white people of people of color who existed already...

No, Western Civilization is not founded on white supremacy at all. It allows people to live freely...

So, like, trans folks should be able to exist as who they are?

It is a civilization that freed slaves...

But not the civilization that held slaves?

It is a civilization that brought you that iPhone. A fundamental role in Western Civilization is that of male and female, and I believe that is very important in terms of what we teach children and how we rear children, very important as to how we jail people. If we're going to define pronouns and change the entire fabric of that makeup, then how many genders are there?

This guy was, very intentionally, missing the point.

It's not a new thing. Look at Roman mythology or Hinduism or anything out of your white—I assume you're Christian, right?
Yeah.
There are a lot of texts that are very, very old that talk about a lot of different types of people...

Speaking of old ways of being, we broached the etymology of the word "hermaphrodite" and how most of the intersex community preferred not using it, as it's often been used in dehumanizing depictions of our community, rooted in bigotry and painting a false picture of who we actually are. This teed Crowder up to deliver what I'll credit as his best zinger of the day:

Yesterday's medical term is today's hate speech and society can't keep up. That's why gender matters, that's why biological studies matters.
You think it's so hard for those people and not the people being marginalized?
Yes.

I started getting up; this was hopeless.

I appreciate having had this conversation, I really do. I'm sorry I don't have a box of tissues for you.

I walked out of the camera's view as he continued to yell behind me about Simone de Beauvoir in 1949 and Judith Butler in the '80s and '90s, nonsensically citing the roots of gender theory as I exited the scene. Danielle and I parted ways, me shaking with anger, to return to more productive uses of our time. As we headed back to our lives, we had no idea this was not just the end of a face-to-face discussion but the beginning of an online conversation that would incite millions of reactions across the globe and that our lives would truly never be the same.

Within hours, Crowder had tagged me in an Instagram post that sicced hoards of neo-Nazis my direction (this was before his following broke one million on the platform, but there were still plenty of rabid bigots thirsty for my blood). The comments on my posts and DMs flooded in by the thousands; then they discovered I had a website with a contact form, so the hate started arriving to my email inbox too. Some messages were more innocuous, just relaying that I was a terrible human, ruining society, and destined for eternal damnation—or asserting that I was lying about being intersex for attention. Others were downright scary—credible-sounding threats of bodily harm, or super weird ones telling me they wanted to choke and rape me in a back alley before running me over with a truck, chopping me up into little pieces, putting me in the microwave, and feeding me to their cat.

Then, the alt-right decided a clip from our conversation was perfect fodder for their paid media advertising across the country, and I started showing up in ads on unrelated YouTube videos nationwide . . . fun.

In the wake of all of this, things got really dark. I also did receive a lot of fan mail and support against the trolls, including the poem that gives the next chapter its title; I don't want to downplay that. But the experience of "reading the comments" taught me the need to create cross-cultural dialogue, even if it's not always neat and tidy or "civil"—as the Right likes to lay claim to, meanwhile fundamentally negating our basic rights and reality—or even necessarily safe. People like me—that is, white people, including cis women and those of us with significant passing privilege, like myself—need to utilize our privilege and step outside of our comfort zones. It will almost always be safer for us to do so than for our nonwhite and trans counterparts. If Janet Mock can talk about being pretty as a privilege—if a Black, trans woman can acknowledge privilege in this capacity—then we sure as hell can. Plus, coming from someone who doesn't look too far off from Tomi Lahren, my words hit the opposing camp differently than they would from other messengers.

That doesn't mean it's easy . . . Danielle and I have dissected the difference in responses to her conversation versus mine, and they are very illustrative: most viewers find her to be at least a *polite* abomination, so more palatable and worthy of commendation. Despite the fact that they believe her to be "sick in the head," her demure attitude is less of a threat to their toxic masculinity than my brazen one, which doesn't fit their perception of how a woman should show up in the world. While labeling me hysterical, they view Danielle as wrong but rational because in their eyes—per many YouTube comments—"she's a man." ("Holy shit, at least they got my pronouns right!" Danielle exclaimed, laughing grimly as we first pored over the online vitriol.)

Beyond the flagrant transphobia, something more subtle was evident. The comment commandos didn't see Danielle as a real woman so threw much less misogyny her way. In Danielle's words: "An uncomfortable truth is I'm a middle aged transgender lesbian. I didn't get as much of the hate that came from that video, because the people who watched the video and who were spewing the hate don't see me as a woman. A lot of the compliments were like, 'Wow, I really like Danielle, because he was really respectful and logical because clearly he's a man,' as if it's a positive thing! The patriarchy is real. So I didn't [suffer as much vitriol] because they think I'm still part of their club. How messed up is that?

"Alicia dealt with so much more hatred than I did, which is just tragic, because her femininity was never challenged by them. But Alicia is an attractive young woman who is also brilliant and fierce, and as a result, so many of the haters had to reconcile with that. That speaks volumes to what we're trying to unpack in the world. . . . When I talk to my ex-wife about it, we just laugh and roll our eyes and say, 'Welcome to the patriarchy!' There's something about being a woman of a certain age that changes the conversation in ways that are complex. Because I'm not really seen by many of these men as an object of desire, I don't put up with as much crap, either."

Danielle was misgendered, suffering that particular brand of willful "misunderstanding" (bigotry). I, on the other hand, was deemed "hot" and thus incited a different type of violence in their responses to my segment—something sexual assault survivors, or anyone who's been sexually harassed in any capacity, will understand well. I was "rude" to Crowder and didn't know my place—which, apparently, is to passively accept someone's denial of my basic existence and to, literally and figuratively, take it lying down.

The one feeble light in all of this, though—a candle's flame in a hurricane, really—was that millions of people now knew that people like me walked this earth among them. In the comments were conversations in the realm of "Wait, if I think Alicia is hot—and she has XY chromosomes—does that make me gay?" The wokest of woke will laugh at how problematic that is, but it shows people pausing to consider their basic conception of sex, gender, and sexuality. They are at the very least exhibiting enough curiosity to question some kind of fundamental "truth" they'd been taught about how and with whom they were supposed to experience attraction. If they watched the video long enough, they might also start to question why.

This wasn't the only time I stepped outside of the algorithmically conditioned echo chambers that are Instagram and TikTok to reach new audiences. Similar to how I was unaware of Crowder's reputation when I first sat down with him, baby activist Alicia once interviewed with a press rep from an agency that worked on placements in a broad variety of publications—not properly considering where and how my message might be portrayed. Our conversation not only ended up in the *Daily Mail*—with an average daily readership of 2.18 million the year it was published—but in a widespread social media push on the publication's platforms as well.

The *Daily Mail* article was titled "Intersex person born with a vagina and testes that were removed in infancy says she used to pretend to have her period to fit in at school but no longer identifies as a 'man or a woman' despite 'looking female,'" which is truly unhinged. The social media push used some gross headline to the effect of "Woman Born with Testicles and Vagina," which is definitely not what you'd prefer to appear plastered all over the internet next to your face. (Though after watching Netflix's *Harry & Meghan* documentary, I realize that being unhappy with how I was represented in the *Daily Mail* puts me in pretty good company.)

Intersex people have, unfortunately, gotten used to a level of exploitation in the struggle for our humanity that often strips us of our humanity in the process. But appearing in paid media pushes by outlets like the *Daily Mail*—and even whatever alt-right publications where Crowder gets airtime, whose names I have no desire to know—is necessary too. It is in these instances that we reach folks who really need to hear our message, holding out hope that one day they might change. I myself grew up calling feminists "feminazis" and even made racist and homophobic jokes in my youth. I'm not proud of it, but I'm here to acknowledge that people are often the product of the structures they're raised in until they witness something different.

Yes, some people are ignorant assholes and will stubbornly

remain ignorant assholes no matter how many chances you give them. I know this firsthand, as—after years of heated Thanksgiving table discussions and going to war on social media feeds—my nuclear family has had to disown some of my aunts, uncles, and cousins who continue to support Trump, despite constant exposure to the work of people like me whom his rhetoric targets and policies harm. But we also have to give folks the opportunity to live up to Maya Angelou's famous assurance to Oprah Winfrey that once we know better, we do better.

We have to keep penetrating deep into these scary spaces where we might find folks who also hold the identities we're uplifting but who haven't been exposed to people like us, who claim those parts of ourselves openly and with pride. And we have to recognize that it'll take a critical mass of changed minds within these communities before certain people will feel safe enough to show their own true colors. Not everyone's willing to expose themselves as a sitting duck but some will surprise us with their support, once they feel like part of a pack; many of these folks might already be farther along in their learning journeys than we think. Crowder viewers, and other participants in similar mob mentalities, might deride us at first—perhaps forever—but I am a firm believer in the power that each of us has to change. And however they process, or don't process, the information I've provided, at the very least these people now know that there are people like me in the world.

They know I ExyST. One day everyone else will too. Every time I fill out a medical form, buy a plane ticket, or am forced to select a next-best option of "F" or "M" on whichever daily drop-down we're notoriously absent from, I feel the sting of our gener-alized erasure from society and am reminded of how much work we have left to do. In the face of death by a thousand paper cuts, I have to breathe deeply and remind myself that I am very much alive. Navigating life in a world designed as if we don't, in fact, reside in it, intersex people have to be really certain—confirmed by the scars on our bodies and in our minds—that we really do. Recognition is the most basic of steps in the fight for our equal rights as human beings, but we need to start somewhere. Crowder claims we didn't change his mind, but I know we planted many seeds that day. If seeing is believing, nearly twenty million views on a problematic piece of political theater—memorialized on an inflammatory bigot's YouTube channel—is a start.

POEM

eres prosa salvaje	*you are wild prose*
eres fuerza y eres lucha	*you are strength and you are struggle*
eres belleza en muchas maneras	*you are beauty in many ways*

VICENTE

eres prosa salvaje
eres fuerza y eres lucha
eres belleza en muchas maneras

You are wild prose. This is a pretty apt description of how I've learned to express myself, whether in written or spoken form, in response to perceived threats to my safety and autonomy. It's how I tear into those whose "civil disagreement" with my existence seeks to erase me and those I care about; as one of the comments on Crowder's YouTube asserted, I had "gutted him like a fish." The three lines that kick off this chapter are poetry, though, not prose. They're an excerpt from an email someone in Peru sent me—a gentler response to the video than I've received from perhaps anyone else:

Dear Alicia,

My name is Vicente and I am writing to you from Lima!

During your discussion with Steven Crowder ("Change My Mind"), I was touched by what I perceive was a clear feeling of frustration/disappointment (from your side) over the prejudices and misunderstandings that many people face. Sometimes people are treated as "anomalies" even though we are humans. I guess it might be emotionally costly to explain "one's case" and still face lack of respect or empathy.

Even though I do not agree with you in some matters, I was touched by you. I wrote a poem and I dedicate it to you. Original is in Spanish (my mother tongue) but I am also adding an English translation, which you can read at the end of this message.

You are brave and beautiful, Alicia.

Warm regards,
Vicente

Belleza en espectro
Para Alicia

Soportas una roca en tu espalda
y aún así caminas.
Has encontrado la fuerza

para enfrentar la sequía aún en primavera;

y has sonreído para celebrar la vida misma.

Has sido el bello verso

que muchos no comprendieron;

eres prosa salvaje,

eres fuerza y eres lucha,

eres belleza en muchas maneras.

Beauty in spectrum
For Alicia

You hold a rock on your back

and yet you walk.

You have found the strength

to face the drought even in spring;

and you have smiled to celebrate life itself.

You have been the beautiful verse

that many did not comprehend;

you are wild prose,

you are strength and you are struggle,

you are beauty in many ways.

You hold a rock on your back and yet you walk. The rock was feeling heavier each passing day ... on top of all the hate emails, DMs, comments, etc., I was still running a City Council campaign, one of the most grueling things one can choose to do even if one is *not* also being targeted by alt-right smear tactics. The lack of sleep and the high stakes, the fact that everyone on the campaign reported directly to me, that we were fighting an uphill battle against a deep-seated and well-funded incumbent—it was all getting to me. Plus, when I knocked on doors to get out the vote, some of the folks who answered recognized me from the Crowder video; never knowing whether the stranger whose threshold I appeared in might actually know who I was and in fact believe that I should be murdered in one of the brutal ways folks recommended online was a whole different level of stress …

My mental health was wearing thin, and I wasn't coping well. I'd long since given up my running routine, citing a lack of time and energy, though I still managed to drink copious amounts at campaign-related events. In my attempt to continually numb or escape from the heaviness of my current reality, one of my lowest moments was taking acid from people I didn't know well and experiencing what I recognize, in hindsight, to be a full psychotic break.

I don't blame the substance—psychedelics have been hugely helpful in my healing journey and connecting with my intuition over the course of many years. But anyone who's partaken knows that the course of your "trip" always depends on your setting, the people you're with, and your mental state at the time. At that point I was in no position to be flooding my body with a powerfully evocative psychoactive substance and certainly not with the individuals who offered it to me; I don't remember a lot but do recall losing my shoes at some point during the night, almost being hit by a car, and waking up more scared for myself and my well-being than ever before or since.

Motivated by that fear, and seeking to regain a sense of control and connection amidst the helplessness I was feeling, I sent the following text out to many fellow activists in my network that morning:

Hello fellow warrior and beautiful human,

We are all in the struggle, and the struggle is real. Their movement is to erase our existence; recently, that came too close to reality for me.

It helped me realize, though, that not only can I not let them win—for others and their lives, but for mine too. Each of our inherent worths is much more than just the piece we are adding to the big puzzle we're solving.

And I appreciate you, not just in the big work you're doing for all of us, but as a human.

I hope to be more intentional moving forward about not losing sight of this, and the first step is me saying hello in this moment of refresh. Thank you for all you do, and thank you for being you. I feel grateful to know you.

A big hug, -A

After hitting send on that text, I dialed Danielle. I told her I needed the day off to recover—explicitly leaving out what I needed to recover from—and hopped in a car with three of my girlfriends to visit Krause Springs, a well-known Hill Country swimming hole some thirty miles west of town. Upon arriving at the idyllic location, a profound paranoia set in. What could have been an escape from the hustle and bustle of daily campaign activities quickly turned into a nightmare, as my anxiety-addled mind convinced me that the farther I was outside of the relative safety of Austin's blue bubble, the greater the chance folks might recognize me from Crowder's video. My friends tried to talk me down, to reassure me that they were by my side and I should crack a cool beer and enjoy the warm sun. I stuck close to them the whole afternoon and returned home that evening feeling more drained than before our "relaxing" day trip.

Rather than pausing to acknowledge my fragile mental state and seek help, I assessed that breaks from the grind didn't prove restful at that point and therefore didn't serve the campaign's success. I threw myself even more deeply into work, and the rest of the summer of 2018 passed in a frenzied blur. I remember very little besides taking a brief pause in August to attend a rally in Chicago organized by Sean Saifa Wall and Pidgeon Pagonis of the Intersex Justice Project, protesting medical malpractice at Lurie Children's Hospital.

That was my first time being around so many intersex people, including heavy-hitters like Kimberly Zieselman—then the head of the important advocacy organization interACT and in 2022 appointed as a State Department advisor for LGBTQ and intersex rights within the Biden Administration—and Hanne

Gaby Odiele, whose story had compelled me to come out in the first place. Unfortunately, I was so all-consumed by the minutiae of our City Council race back home that I barely got to connect with the broad array of intersex folks who'd flown in from across the country to show support. Some of the attendees have since expressed that they perceived me as aloof, at the time deeming myself more important than the other activists; in actuality, I was hyperfixated on events elsewhere, meanwhile exhibiting symptoms of severe burnout.

By October, I was running on fumes. One weekend morning, I was headed to our campaign headquarters to train and send our supporters out to knock on doors throughout the community. It was a beautiful morning, cooler than it had been in Austin for quite some time, so on my way into the office I took a quick detour to pick up a couple of gallons of hot coffee for our canvassers. I lugged the jugs into my beat-up Prius, pressed the ignition button, tuned to my go-to NPR affiliate, and heard the words "The Trump Administration is planning changes to federal civil rights laws that would define sex as either male or female, unchangeable, and determined by the genitals a person is born with." The reporter continued that any confusion would be clarified through genetic testing. Tears started rolling down my face as I drove the few remaining blocks between Starbucks and campaign HQ.

NPR referenced this as a blow to transgender rights, and it was. But amid all this, the fate of intersex people—yet again—seemed to have been forgotten. Our community being left out of conversations directly affecting our rights (often more directly, even, than queer or trans folks) is something I've unfortunately grown numb to. But I hadn't yet developed that coping mechanism at the time. Combined with months of sleep deprivation and too much caffeine, the volatile combination proved to be too much. I pulled into the driveway at HQ, placed the car in park, and fell out of the door sobbing hot wet tears on the ground. Danielle observed this absurd and concerning scene through the front window and rushed to me, demanding to know whether or not I was okay. "I really don't think so," I slurred as mucus poured into my mouth.

"We need to talk," Danielle said, "but given that folks are literally pulling up now, I am going to ask you to compose yourself, get in the car, and sit this shift out. Please either wait in your car until folks have been sent out to walk blocks or until you feel well enough to drive back to your place, and I'll check on you then." I'd never felt so unprofessional in my life but also had never cared less. I was experiencing grief, but at the time I couldn't identify that; all I could identify was rage. And that rage needed to pour out of my fingers.

Once I settled my heaving breaths to a pace and intensity I felt comfortable driving with, I sped back to my apartment, ready to write out the millions of thoughts and feelings flooding through me. I didn't know where they'd go yet, or if anyone would listen. But I knew I needed them out of my body where they felt corrosive. I couldn't handle any more negativity inside me; spilling it onto (online) paper was the only option that seemed like it made sense. So I vomited my soul into a piece about intersex invisibility—and erasure from the conversations about our own erasure—all in the course of about forty-five minutes. At that point I felt a lot more clear. *Who do I know who has connections at the* New York Times?*... Ah, Jacob.*

Jacob Tobia is a friend of mine I was blessed to first meet at SXSW. You might know their story from their incredible memoir *Sissy: A Coming-of-Gender Story*, their voice as the character Double Trouble in the cartoon *She-Ra and the Princesses of Power*, or at least their unforgettable aesthetic from Instagram. We met through mutual friends from their past life as a budding politico before switching into primarily media work, and I knew they'd written for the *Times* before. The best thing about Jacob is that we might not talk for months and then reunite in Austin as if no time has passed for a boozy brunch with sex writers like Zachary Zane (aka The Boyslut) followed by midday dancing in a cowboy boot store on South Congress. This time I was seeking press contacts instead of tequila shots, and sensing my urgency, Jacob came through in an instant. They introduced me to a woman at the *New York Times* named Alicia—perfect. And she was based in London, so at that point it was Monday morning for her and she received my email right away—even more perfect. Sometimes when something's meant to happen, the stars just align.

The piece that arose from my collapse onto Danielle's driveway had somehow morphed into a "fuck you" letter to Donald Trump titled "Intersex, and Erased Again" that first ran in the *Times* on October 23, 2018—three days before Intersex Awareness Day. The piece catapulted my online profile in a much more positive way than the Crowder conversation had, given the *Times*'s significantly more liberal readership versus a hoard of online far-right trolls. It garnered me nationwide attention from educators, other activists, even the likes of fellow former cojones-holder Lance Armstrong. It generated a groundswell of local support too, enabling me to organize Austin's historic first ever Intersex Awareness Day rally a year later at City Hall. It even earned official proclamations declaring October 26 as Intersex Awareness Day by State Representative Gina Hinojosa and Austin's mayor, who both spoke alongside me and other activists at the rally. A friend of mine also read to the crowd of hundreds of intersectional participants a letter penned by my mom, which was perhaps the most meaningful of all.

Although intersex visibility soared after the piece's publication, our City Council campaign unfortunately didn't generate the necessary awareness for us to win at the polls. Despite a strong push to the finish line, executed by a broad coalition of volunteers who believed in our vision—from students to urbanist policy nerds to those who simply believed that Austin needed and deserved more diverse representation—we suffered a loss just a few days later. After nearly a year of backbreaking hustle and personal investment, seven days a week and drawing on every fiber of our beings, losing our race was devastating. I was emotionally disheartened and physically burned out. It was a level of disappointment I'd never experienced before and probably haven't since. But for the sake of everyone who'd given their all for us, we tried to keep some perspective on the bigger picture in the wake of our defeat.

Though we had failed to win a seat at the city level, we'd moved the needle on trans and intersex issues on a much larger scale. We had broken down many walls and served as a bridge between many different communities, so I and our core campaign staff tattooed matching bridges on our ankles in commemoration of the campaign's logo and the time now imprinted into our memories forever. Ultimately, we were proud—proud and exhausted. Danielle would go back to building physical bridges as an engineer, and I would cinch a role at an investment fund in town whose founders had supported both our campaign and Wendy's organization—but first we all needed to let off some serious steam. I decided to push back the start date at my new job till January 2019 and flew overseas to visit some friends in Europe, including a fellow intersex activist I'd met before only online, Suz Temko.

My experience meeting Suz in a dimly lit bar in Amsterdam is one that only a fellow intersex activist will understand. Queer and trans folks can surely relate to encountering in person for the first time someone you've met only online whose identity is similar to yours in ways you've determined in perhaps a niche Facebook group or targeted dating app. There's a feeling of instant kinship. The intersex experience is that on steroids; my fellow intersex activist friend Val Hill coined it "intersynergy." While many cities and even smaller rural towns at this point have LGBTQIA+ communities that are established or at least budding, it is still rare to find intersex folks who are out among them. Living in a state as large as Texas (which, I can tell you, takes a long-ass time to drive across and actually used to be its own country), I can count on only one hand the number of intersex activists I know. You may often hear stories of lesbians driving long distances to meet someone, just for one date; with intersex folks, you'll fly across an ocean just for a friendly hang.

Suz and I spent just a couple of days together in the Dutch country that happens to be Texas's largest trading partner in the EU—a fact I now know, having met with the Netherlands' queen on a diplomatic mission to the Lone Star State just a few years later. But I can remember never having felt so seen as I was in Suz's presence, perhaps because—in addition to being intersex—she and I apparently grew up fifteen minutes from each other for part of our childhoods. It was somehow comforting to know that little fourth-grade Alicia wasn't as alone as she thought she was, even geographically. We also shared a lot of the same doctors, something intersex folks often find in the "six degrees of Kevin Bacon" game that we ultimately end up playing with our healthcare providers—linking together a network that proves vital in understanding our own medical histories and advocating for better services moving forward.

This whole phase of my life—first owning my identity and then linking up with others who share it—felt very significant. I felt the familiar pressing need to press these memories into my skin. Just a month after I'd tattooed our campaign bridge on my ankle and a couple months after I'd stamped the Tropic of Capricorn over my scar, I was already ready for more ink. Suz was game, so we partook in some of the city's finest marijuana-laced baked goods and embarked on a literal and metaphorical trip down a drizzly Amsterdam street not far from her home to memorialize our time together at a nearby tattoo parlor.

As I said before, when something is meant to happen, sometimes the universe sends you a sign; stumbling into that tattoo shop, we were greeted by a blond, mustachioed artist who was from the Netherlands but had spent a good amount of time living in Beaumont, Texas. When I told Daan I wanted a tattoo on my finger, he tried to talk me out of it; the ink fades there faster than anywhere else on a body. When I clarified that I needed to tattoo I ExyST on my middle finger specifically—so that if I ever met Donald Trump and in my anger lost the ability to form words, I could still send him the desired message—Daan suddenly changed his tune.

He regaled us with some of the strange characters he'd experienced living in small-town Texas, many of them not the sort of folks you'd want to get as up close and personal with as you do in his profession. A man had once entered Daan's Texas parlor and removed his shirt to reveal a KKK symbol. This man requested a word tattooed across his chest in wood-grain letters, and our new Dutch friend covertly drew little dicks and balls into each of those letters, as a silent protest for having to even touch let alone ink this Klan member's skin. That was the wrong parlor for that Klansman to have stumbled into years before, but it was certainly the right artist for me to have happened to meet on that chilly evening in the Netherlands.

Suz also got a tattoo, so despite the fact that we haven't seen each other since and don't talk much either, I remain inextricably bonded to her. Tattoo or not, I feel this way with pretty much every intersex person I've ever met. For most of our lives, we have "*been the beautiful verse that many did not comprehend*"— yet in the instant of meeting someone who shares our lived experience, they already know the lyrics; within moments, we're singing together in harmony.

After a brief stint in northern Italy to visit some other friends who once lived in the region, I returned to the States, finally refreshed and ready to face some other demons of mine. The night we lost Danielle's race, I drank too much at our own campaign party to offer her any real support. I ultimately left early, unable to bear the psychological burden of our loss and leaving Danielle to fend for herself. When I reached out to her in the wee hours of the following morning to apologize and request that we meet, the compassionate insomniac that she is immediately responded in agreement. The Magnolia Cafe where she and I met at around 5 a.m. that morning on Lake Austin Boulevard no longer exists, but I'll always remember sitting across from her in silence, both of us staring into our black coffees—the color of everything we were struggling to process inside and certainly couldn't put into words. Although we couldn't yet speak to the campaign, we both had things we wanted to get off our chests:

I'm really sorry for leaving early last night . . . I feel like I let the campaign down, but more than anything I let you down as a friend.

I'm not going to lie, it was pretty shitty. But you've gone above and beyond as both a colleague and a friend in more ways than one since I've met you. You know you're family at this point; one night doesn't erase any of that. Speaking of friendship, though, I wanted to discuss a friend of mine with you. It's something I've been wanting to talk to you about for some time, actually, but wanted to wait until the race had run its course.

She paused. I continued to stare into my coffee.

This friend of mine is bipolar. And that's a very powerful thing—scary, yes, but also it can be a real asset sometimes. It's kind of the mad genius effect. When he's bad, it's real bad, but when he's manic—well, he has started and run successful companies and really done well for himself. I see some of that in you too.

Danielle: another pause; me: more coffee staring.

You are definitely a genius too; no one has any doubt about that. But besides that trait, I also see some of the same behaviors in you that I see in him—when you send emails at odd hours because you haven't slept in a long time, when you're clearly worn down but convinced that the only thing that can make you feel better is going out for a long run, when you talk so fast that no one else can properly understand or process what you're saying and then you get frustrated that we can't keep up ... does any of that sound right to you?

This time I looked up to meet her gaze.

Of course. That's me in a nutshell.

And has any of that ever felt like a problem to you? Like something you couldn't control?

Definitely. I never told you about the night before I took the day off the campaign to go to Krause Springs with my girls but it got pretty dark. I had taken some acid but that wasn't exactly the problem—sometimes acid's been great for me, like when I ate some with two of my friends from Brazil at the top of Mount Tamalpais and the spirits of women across time told me it was my turn to help lead the reproductive rights movement in the South and then we almost got attacked by a bunch of coyotes...

Well that certainly sounds like quite the story, but let's stick to the topic at hand...

Right. Well, I think the acid kind of heightened what was happening but it was a feeling—a mode, a way of operating—that had been engaged for a while at that point; the drugs just intensified it.

Got it. And what was that feeling like?

Well, I hadn't slept in days, and everything felt overwhelming. The closest experience I can remember to it was when I was preparing to move to Africa. The travel medicine doctor I saw had given me a few options for antimalarials, and one of them was being on antibiotics long term, which I didn't want for a variety of reasons, and the other was super expensive. So she told me there was a third option that was significantly cheaper but also had very severe mental health effects on a small portion of folks who take it—so she wanted me to try a larger dose than normal while I was still stateside so she could observe me, rather than being unpleasantly surprised overseas. The regular dose was supposed to be a pill once a week, but she had me take one three days in a row—which apparently for the majority of people wouldn't do much, but for me, it turned me pretty insane. I didn't sleep for about a week, was doing push-ups every hour on the hour at weird hours of the night. I ended up drinking too much because I was honestly just trying to get tired enough to sleep and things got bad then too.

It sounds like you were pretty manic.

Yeah, that's what my research on that drug said, actually. I didn't end up taking it in Africa, obviously—I shelled out for the more expensive option to avoid being out of my mind on a foreign continent. But some soldiers in the Vietnam War took it, and apparently a small portion of them went insane. They took it once a week and came up with terms like "Whako Wednesday" or "Psycho Sunday" to describe their experience. Or as Prince coined after the fact, Manic Monday...

Wow. Well I came here to try to open your mind to thinking about something, but it sounds like maybe the topic isn't that foreign to you.

People have often asked me how I do everything that I do—how I manage it all. But they don't see that besides the phases where I accomplish wild stuff—like getting a piece written and placed in the *New York Times* all within a matter of hours—there's a dark side to it too—a depressive side, when I don't want to get off the couch for days.

That all sounds pretty typical of my friend's bipolar experience. I wonder if maybe this is something you want to look into, exploring with the help of people who understand it better than you or I do. I don't think my friend has always necessarily managed it well, and you have such a bright future ahead of you; if you can find a way to harness the strengths that having a brain that works like yours provides while also minimizing the weaknesses, just imagine how powerful you can be.

I think you're right.

These next two months before you start your next job might be just the time to focus some energy on figuring all this out.

When I got back from Europe, I saw a psychiatrist who easily confirmed Danielle's "diagnosis." At the time, I felt fear but also relief in receiving both an explanation for why I am how I am and some suggested pathways to become more how I'd like to be—methods for the madness. A 2017 study in neuropsychiatry titled "Positive Traits in the Bipolar Spectrum: The Space between Madness and Genius" found that "positive psychological traits of spirituality, empathy, creativity, realism, and resilience are frequently observed in bipolar individuals"; I'd like to think I embody all those traits. The label also puts me in good company with some of the most groundbreaking creatives throughout history, from Vincent van Gogh to Mariah Carey.

Writing this years later, I feel extra motivated to own this aspect of my identity in the wake of Kanye West's recent anti-Semitic remarks so that people understand that being bipolar does not make you a bigoted asshole... that's all on you, boo. It does make you different, and subject to a lot of societal stigma, but that's all territory I already tread. I am intersex *and* I am bipolar.

> *Intersex, middle*
> *Bipolar, extremes*
> *There is no right way to be*
> *except me.*

I penned this poem long after I found the beauty in not just my physical human condition but my mental one too. Admitting to myself and having someone help me identify what I struggle with was just the first step on a long journey of healing. This has also involved figuring out which medications do and don't work for me. As it turns out, alcohol isn't the best medicine to turn to, despite what we've been marketed to believe... Once I found something bigger than myself to commit to, the less inclined I've felt to get super fucked up in general. Plus, alcohol messes with your sleep, which is no bueno for bipolar folks and we'll explore why momentarily.

Ironically—after my acid trip that led to my diagnosis in the first place—psychedelic drugs like mushrooms have proved to be hugely therapeutic for me, at the right dose, especially during depressive phases. Providers are now actively prescribing them for PTSD sufferers and others, though in too limited of a geographic scope. We need to follow in Oregon's footsteps by decriminalizing psilocybin nationwide and then go even further. Not only have hallucinogenic "drugs" been valued as powerful spiritual guides and medicine in a variety of indigenous cultures for ages—meaning these groups therefore bear an outsized burden of criminalization—but society at large is starting to catch up.

Research has shown the benefits of many of these substances in positively rewiring neural pathways to alleviate addictions and promote a greater connection to our environment and ourselves. Speaking of indigenous healing modalities, I had a particularly life-changing experience with sacred medicine deep in the jungle, right after finishing my first draft of this book. Amazonian shamans guided me through multiple ceremonies centered on imbibing *yagé*, a psychoactive and entheogenic brewed drink that tribal leaders have used in rituals to connect with the divine for centuries. While elaborating on this experience would require writing a whole 'nother book, I will say that I gained some truly unique insight into my own psyche over the course of a few days in the Colombian rainforest that I had not yet unearthed through years of talk therapy.

Therapy has been vital, though, in improving how I function in the world as a neurodivergent person—as has the integration of many non-substance-based practices into my day-to-day, like yoga. In fact, as I've become more attuned to my mind and body, I've cut way down on my use of certain substances like weed and booze. Don't get me wrong, I still enjoy a few drinks at a wedding or a THC gummy before dancing at a concert or settling in for a good movie, but I don't use them to numb out anymore. I now embrace the darker sides of my existence, rather than fleeing from them. Carl Jung first popularized "shadow work," which explores sides of ourselves we may have exiled or repressed. Learning not just to accept but truly to love my whole self has been the best medicine. As I expressed in another poem of my own in 2019,

Love more, now.

Ask for help, and give it.
Turn to one another, not substances.
And above all, don't wait till it's too late…

Love more, now.

My healing journey has primarily included nonmedicinal mechanisms for building a life that doesn't propel me into manic and depressive phases—one where I'm living in alignment with how my body naturally works, to the extent that that's possible in late-stage capitalism. It has involved honoring my needs for both ample rest and consistent exercise; it has necessitated building a career outside the traditional nine-to-five. I've also become more able to predict and recognize fluctuations in my energy and mood after finding that such fluctuations are often tied to the moon's phases. It is interesting that, though I don't get a period, the feminine side of my nature has found a way to manifest itself in a somewhat monthly cycle.

This checks out scientifically, as many studies have shown how bipolarity is greatly affected by disruptions of our circadian rhythms. On brighter nights, our restlessness is affected by increased light exposure and greater activity among bugs and animals outside whose noises might also contribute to keeping us awake. This can trigger shifts in our moods and behaviors as, for all humans, proper sleep helps keep us "sane"; the shifts we experience as bipolar people are just greater because we embody more extreme aspects of humanity. Rather than viewing this as a positive or a negative, I like to think that we are simply more in tune with natural variance in the universe's energies—oscillating between the light and the darkness that both exist within and govern us all.

This also checks out culturally, in the widespread belief that "crazies" come out at the full moon and the fact that emergency room visits uptick accordingly. Rather than viewing myself as a "crazy," though, I'd posit that those of us who are bipolar are merely different, and misunderstood. Like how Professor Lupin in the Harry Potter books had to shroud his identity as a werewolf in secrecy to escape shame and stigma but was still one of the best professors our favorite Gryffindor trio ever had. (Note to trigger-happy cancel culturalists: a reference to Harry Potter is *not* an endorsement of J. K. Rowling.) Similar to the plight of a werewolf—also governed by the moon's phases—I've come to recognize that being bipolar is perhaps both my greatest weakness and my greatest strength. I ultimately have grown to see my life's journey as an intersex person in a similar light.

We can all learn to embody and embrace dualities in our

being—you don't have to be bipolar or intersex to do so. As I've mentioned, I'm also a Taurus, with the stubbornness associated with that sign. But the flip side of stubbornness is persistence; I have that in spades too and wouldn't be the activist I am without it. What society tells us makes us weak often is the source of our greatest strength, as long as we have the courage to heal and channel it in positive ways. In vulnerability, there is power. In flaws, there is beauty. This is all succinctly yet profoundly encapsulated in the final lines of the poem that Vicente wrote for me, which now sits on the left hip of this bipolar intersex body of mine: *You are strength and you are struggle. You are beauty in many ways.*

PEACH

It has the juice.
—TARIQ, THE CORN KID, FROM "RECESS THERAPY"

Long before the Corn Kid talked about a "big lump with knobs" having the juice (if you haven't seen the viral video, watch it now), the Presidents of the United States of America sang about how "She's Lump"—whatever that means—as well as a different juicy fruit. Their song "Peaches" was quite the earworm. Apparently it's actually about the interplay of capitalism and socialism. At least that's what I found on Reddit, which we all know *must* mean it's true. After having drained my personal coffers to work on Danielle's campaign, I spent a year rebuilding some stability in my bank account through a job within a capitalist institution. Not that we had run an outright socialist campaign by any means—as an engineer, Danielle had a lot of support from the business community—but the circles I operated in for my new job at a local impact investing fund were very different.

People who help people come at the work with a variety of theories of change. There's certainly room for—and a real need for—all of us. There's a difference, however, between "Band-Aid" work to patch holes within existing systems that were built to keep certain folks down and systemic change focused on up-ending the causes of societal ills at the root. The donors I culti-vated in this new role were less concerned about giving enough to propel candidates to break these systems that don't serve the masses; they sometimes seemed more motivated to act in a way that might generate positive press and a boost to a brand's rep-utation, or give enough to hit certain thresholds that unlock tax breaks... more of a "peaches for me" than "peaches for free" crowd, to put it in the Presidents' lyrical terms.

I was definitely able to help do some good through organiz-ing philanthropitch (philanthropy + pitching) events that raised corporate dollars to support nonprofits in cities across the US. These nonprofits gained much-needed money and visibility for their work; I got to travel again, building my own network in new cities and spheres of influence in order to make that possible. All the while, though, I was working within a system that keeps people reliant on the generosity of the wealthy. I never shook a persistent itch to get back to overhauling that system, in order to ensure a more just and equitable distribution of resources in the first place.

Luckily, I became close with a co-worker of mine, Julie Oliver, who was also killing time between election cycles. She had run for US Congress while I ran Danielle's campaign, and despite her loss, she was gearing up to try again. Julie and I aligned on pretty much everything, including our belief in a single-payer healthcare model, having experienced firsthand how our current system doesn't serve us. When she told me she was looking to leave the fund we both worked for to run a second campaign and try—yet again—to unseat one of the most deplorable Republican incumbents around, I asked her to take me with her.

Julie and I both quit our jobs in early 2021 to get back on the campaign trail, with me serving as her political director. Despite having run Danielle's race, I found that a federal-level campaign was a totally different ball game—with multimillion-dollar stakes and a district that stretched 212 miles from top to bottom. Rather than organizing individuals, I had to mobilize groups that organized individuals, including Democratic Party infrastructure across thirteen counties. To say we were underdogs was an understatement. But Julie had made it from being homeless and a teen mom to becoming a lawyer, healthcare industry exec, and more; if anyone could do it, I believed she could, and it was an honor to be granted the opportunity to try alongside her.

She and I crisscrossed Central Texas, visiting voters everywhere from small-town conservative strongholds to Killeen, a majority Black community adjacent to Fort Hood—the army base where the soldier Vanessa Guillen was harassed and murdered. We even made it down to Mexico, visiting migrant families awaiting asylum trials at the border camps in Matamoros to bring awareness to inhumane policies espoused by our opponent. I got to see the true face of Texas outside the liberal bubble that surrounds our state capital and to understand how they see folks like us. I became even more certain that progressive policies could benefit every Texan, if we could just get past the branding issue that has labeled us as being out of touch with their needs.

It's especially frustrating that we weren't able to scrape by as the incumbent we lost to is someone entirely out of touch with those needs—someone who hoards to feel secure rather than understanding that by sharing with others, we will all be more secure. (Despite what they may believe, I've found the wealthiest in society often exhibit the greatest scarcity mindset.) I wish the impoverished voters in his district understood that true poverty of character; rich as he may be, morally he's bankrupt.

We ultimately lost the race because changing hearts and minds like this takes more than one two-year election cycle. Despite losing the election, though, we didn't give up the fight. Julie has since teamed up with another friend of ours who ran in a different congressional district, Mike Siegel, to found Ground Game Texas. Their organization works to chip away at voter biases over time through engagement on issues everyday people care about, from weed to abortion, and not just when a candidate's race is on the line.

We've continued to show up in rural communities since, taking a trip to Marlin, Texas, in the wake of the now infamous winter storm of early 2021. Never have I seen a town so proud of the life-giving properties of its mineral water, which brought the New

York Giants down for ten seasons in the early twentieth century to bathe in it. Yet it couldn't be consumed—even boiled—so although water flooded the town's streets in the storm's wake, residents were dying of thirst. We took water door-to-door while our state's junior senator, Ted Cruz, flew to Mexico with his family, despite the fact that some of us (myself included) had just regained access to power and running water ourselves. We did it because it's the right thing to do, regardless of whether or not we got elected. Maybe folks will eventually recognize the difference between this approach to community-building and that of those who currently hold power in our state…

It was this approach that motivated us to head to Georgia when we first lost the congressional seat back in November 2020. None of the candidates who'd tried to flip seats from red to blue had won in Central Texas, and we needed something to revive our hope that better was possible. Two runoff elections for US Senate seats a few states over was an excuse to caravan out to assist our southern cousins—to prove that it wasn't worth writing off our entire region. My friend Sri Preston Kulkarni had just run (twice in a row, like Julie and Mike) to attempt to flip a seat in Sugar Land, Texas, outside of Houston, and earned himself a role on now senator Jon Ossoff's campaign team. We had less than two months to secure Ossoff's and fellow Democratic challenger Raphael Warnock's seats, but I packed all the warm clothing I had left from my time living in the Northeast, bought Chiquita some sweaters, and drove out to join him.

Sri is half-Indian and had landed in a house reserved for Asian

American and Pacific Islander (AAPI) organizers. The house is owned by Cam Ashling—chairwoman of the Georgia chapter of the Asian American Action Fund, who came to the US as a refugee from Vietnam in 1988. Her home is entirely, intentionally, overrun with goats. Imagine a quiet road in the wealthy Atlanta suburb of Buckhead, with a sweeping driveway leading up to a stone-clad mansion. Now picture the entire front lawn covered in bleating animals and the halls filled with Asian organizers from across the country with a broad range of ethnic backgrounds who had converged upon this urban farm with a singular purpose. All that, plus me—the random, intersex white girl from Texas who'd been invited to stay as a guest of Sri's and who was to earn her keep by feeding the goats plus the chickens Cam kept out back. I also made a goat yoga video on Instagram to try to recruit more Texans to join us.

We spent our days at a frantic pace, knocking on doors across various regions of Atlanta and nearby cities and executing outreach to bring more volunteers and dollars on board. At night, we'd congregate back at the goat house to host K-pop dance parties in our pajamas and share food from the variety of cultures represented in our ranks. Eventually, we needed all hands on deck to expand the reach of our efforts and took to staying in hotels in far-reaching corners of the state. Julie and her daughter even came out to meet us in Savannah, along with several other Texas politicos we'd convinced to make the trip out East. We met Georgians of every background imaginable, but I remember Shaira's story, in the tiny town of Thomaston, as particularly emblematic of what kept us going at warp speed.

Shaira is a sixty-something-year-old Black woman with locs dyed the color of red velvet, as she put it. She had made various requests for a mail-in ballot, as she wanted to avoid being exposed to COVID at the polls—having suffered a stroke in 2016 and struggled with high blood pressure and diabetes since. The ballot never came, and she wasn't surprised. "They didn't want to hear from me," she told me, tears in her eyes, "but my life really is dependent on this so I'm going to put my life in jeopardy to vote. I'm going to go out there and take a chance and head to the civic center and chance catching COVID because they've got their foot on my neck but they're not going to suppress me."

When I asked Shaira whether she'd voted before, she told me that she had felonies in her record and hadn't been able to vote for six decades—including for Barack Obama—but finally got to cast her first ballot against Trump in 2020. "I've seen some things, 'specially here in Georgia in a rural town, so I got something to say with my vote. I never got that feeling before, but now I feel it and I like it."

Shaira asked me why she couldn't vote on Monday, and I told her that it was because early voting had ended. She had to wait until the next day—Election Day proper. I told her that she was given the wrong voting date on purpose and that I'd had to correct several of her neighbors. "If they're doing this to a little old nobody like me, not sending me a ballot," she pondered. "They're trying to stop ME from voting? That really inspires me to show up and do it. They're trying to scare me, trying to stop me. It's not gonna be that easy. I don't have religion but I have faith; I have faith this is not gonna work. We DO have a say."

At that point I was in tears. I made sure Shaira knew to show up on the fifth, not the fourth, and gave her an extra face mask emblazoned with the word "VOTE" on it to help protect her. I gathered my campaign literature and left her porch as she called out to me, "Tell every heaux you know!" I'll never forget Shaira. She was the first person I thought of when both Warnock—a Black Georgian like her—and Ossoff won a few days later. This win was momentous not just for residents of the Peach State like Shaira, but for all Americans and, frankly, the world.

Just shy of two years later, Senator Warnock landed in another runoff election against Trump-backed candidate Herschel Walker—who actively bullied trans kids to try to secure the vote. (At a rally in Calhoun, he told the crowd that trans children wouldn't get into heaven because Jesus wouldn't recognize them.) Warnock squeaked by with 51 percent of the vote, but the work is obviously not done in Georgia; the closeness of that race, and Stacey Abrams's loss a month before, shows that democracy is a never-ending responsibility that requires our frequent and unrelenting participation. But at the time, we had flipped the balance of power in one of the most powerful governing bodies on the planet, enabling better federal votes on everything from basic human rights to climate change for at least the next couple of years—and we had done it earning one citizen's vote at a time.

Results came out showing that the number of votes that had tipped the election in our favor was in the range of the number of new AAPI voters who had turned out to polls. Our team's work had made it happen. The media was starting to take note, as did the political powers that be. President Biden's administration appointed Sri to a leadership position at AmeriCorps, and my friend Chantale Wong, who'd become a new auntie to me over the course of our two months in Georgia, was named the US Executive Director of the Asian Development Bank—the first openly queer person, not to mention Chinese immigrant woman, to ever hold an ambassadorial level role in the US government. Like after Danielle's campaign, I got a tattoo to commemorate my experience in Georgia, which had also left a lifelong mark on me. Upon my return to Austin, a queer woman of color artist, Dot Sheridan, inked a tiny peach on the back of my left arm.

The peach symbolized Georgia but also a transformational shift in my activism. After winning in Georgia—my first time *not* losing a campaign—I felt a sense of permission to take a step back from electoral politics again, at least for the time being. Running campaigns is brutal. I have utmost respect for those who continue to make it their life's work, but my own energy wasn't what it had been. I needed a break and wanted to continue to support these efforts while also engaging in work that felt less draining— work where I could see returns on my labor a lot sooner than we'd be able to in Texas politics. I decided to pivot away from what drains my cup and help fill mine and that of others by flaunting my peach in a different way...

Pleasure Activism: The Politics of Feeling Good is a collection of essays by Black doula and writer Adrienne Maree Brown, focused on how we can tap into our emotional and erotic desires to organize against oppression. Intersex people have been so desexualized by society that I saw this new approach as extra empowering. By reminding myself and showing others that intersex people are, in fact, hot—not just brave—I could reclaim a beautiful aspect of humanity that had been taken from us. I'd stripped down for an Instagram photo back in Georgia, wearing pink panties we'd received as a gift to the campaign that had "My Vote Is My Voice" stamped in red right on the tush. No one else in our house had wanted to touch the underwear, believing the delivery was inappropriate. But the silky panties felt good on my skin and made me feel good in my skin. Plus, I saw them as another path to engaging voters, urging folks in the caption to "Get that 🍑 to the polls on Tuesday!"

So much of campaign messaging comes across as stilted and inauthentic. The Right, for better or worse, is better at tugging on voters' heartstrings—appealing to core aspects of humanity, in their case usually bitterness and resentment. Human beings are sexual, unless they're asexual, despite what our Puritanical culture in the US would lead us to believe. Regardless of folks' feelings on the Kardashians, they have undoubtedly paved the way for women to be able to embrace their sexuality and be successful—as have many other pop culture icons, from Megan Thee Stallion and Cardi B to Miley Cyrus. Everyone has always told me I sound like Miley Cyrus (let me be clear: I was born first, so *she* sounds like *me*), so maybe it was time for me to start creating a path for the public to understand that political women could be sexual beings too. In a world where the mix of sex and politics usually leads to disgrace and scandal, it seemed about time for some positive representation in that realm. As an intersex person who'd already had to fight being desexualized by doctors who told me I was undesirable for how I was born, I felt well-suited to be this messenger.

Since then, I've seen a budding movement surrounding this work—from former *Maxim* model Alejandra "Ali" Campoverdi running for congress in California's 34th district and former stripper Alexandra Hunt running in Philadelphia's 3rd to my friend Becky Bullard's Democrasexy website promoting Texas politics. A lot of women will tell us we're setting things back for our fight to be taken seriously—like when Wendy, a feminist hero, once told me my skirt was too short before I entered the Capitol for a legislative hearing. I beg to differ.

If Donald Trump can get elected president of the United States after bragging about grabbing women by the pussy, I should sure as hell be able to succeed in political activism while also exercising my right to engage in *consensual* sex. In my mind, this is as vital a part of winning our body autonomy as securing reproductive rights or ending human trafficking. And if I start to forget that—in the face of pushback rooted in internalized misogyny, from well-intentioned but self-hating individuals of any gender—I have a nice juicy peach on my arm to remind me of the nice juicy peach behind me that hustled itself all over Georgia and won.

This boost in my confidence was bigger than just showing my booty. It meant no longer conforming to a model of what activism was "supposed" to look like and hoping things would change; it meant owning my own model of what activism *could* look like and *being* the change. In the past, I had attended galas like those hosted by the Human Rights Campaign and left early in tears—frustrated that despite years of begging, intersex people *still* failed to be mentioned let alone incorporated into the organization's work. Now, I attended galas hosted by Planned Parenthood with trans icon Laverne Cox as the guest of honor, and when she discussed health inequities and the violation of rights faced by her community, I shouted out from the audience "and intersex people too." One of the event organizers, a prominent member of our Travis County Democratic Party, scolded me afterward for disrupting the peace, but Laverne applauded me in front of the crowd and invited me to take a photo backstage. Apparently, communities that have had to throw bricks to survive—like at the original Stonewall Riots—understand the concept of building your own table when no one invites you to theirs.

The fact that some progressives prevent intersex activists from being included in conversations that affect our bodies has been part of the problem. Not just in Texas, but in states across the country, bills meant to harm trans folks often include a specific loophole that pertains to intersex bodies. While blocking surgeries and hormones for trans children, legislation almost always includes clauses that allow for the continuation of these operations on intersex children despite a lack of consent. We're often referred to using hypermedicalized terminology, though, like having "disorders of sex development"—or referenced in coded language, like a list of specific intersex variations most folks are unfamiliar with—rather than including the word "intersex" outright. Because of this, and the generalized lack of awareness of our community, most people don't realize that these bills are as much about intersex kids as they are about trans kids.

Unfortunately, though, even when we explain this to LGBTQIA+ orgs, reproductive rights groups, and the broader progressive organizing community, they often refrain from including us in their work because they feel it complicates the message or detracts from their ability to adequately protect trans youth. While it's true that the government should listen to the parents and doctors of trans kids who have actively sought affirming care, circumstances are different for intersex children in that medical procedures are foist upon us when we are too young to participate in conversations surrounding these decisions—let alone to have developed any sense of bodily autonomy and understanding of how to enforce it.

It's easier for advocates to make a blanket statement that "these surgeries don't happen on children" rather than specifying that although it's indeed rare to operate on trans minors, these surgeries *are* often enacted on intersex infants and youth but without our consent. This incomplete message might fit more easily in a news headline but it erases the lived experience of people like me and leaves a whole class of young people open to harm. How long must intersex kids be thrown under the bus for the sake of some perceived piecemeal progress?

The message really isn't very complicated, so I'm going to spell it out here:

The bills that block gender-affirming care for trans kids who *want* that care allow parents to force these same procedures on intersex kids who haven't asked for them. As VICE News so adequately put it: "Republicans have compared gender-affirming health care to child abuse and Nazi war crimes. But they're more than happy to let doctors perform surgeries on intersex children." The Republican machine has adopted "grooming" as a favorite talking point, claiming that drag-queen story hours and the liberal politicians who permit them to take place are forcing children into LGBTQIA+ "lifestyles." Meanwhile, by passing legislation that permits forcibly altering intersex kids' bodies without their consent—to align them with an "M" or "F" gender, different from the sex they were naturally born into—*they* are, in fact, grooming kids to be trans.

These bills are as hypocritical as they are nonsensical. They're not rooted in logic or what's healthiest for children. They're merely enforcing what is considered normal in the eyes of some elected officials. These legislators think trans kids are not "normal"; therefore, they block them from being able to realize their true selves. They also think intersex kids are born not "normal," so they allow doctors to force "normalize" our bodies, whether or not we want that to happen. I've testified in enough hearings to this effect to know that the Republicans in Texas's state legislature understand this clear as day—enough so that they warp some of my own language regarding forced sterilizations to support misinformation about trans-affirming care. We need the opposition to catch up; in the words of Martin Luther King Jr., "shallow understanding from people of good will is more frustrating than absolute misunderstanding from people of ill will." Word.

If only the progressive opposition could parrot some of the

language above, it would show how clearly misguided and intentionally malicious the conservatives really are. Even beyond the legislative context, intersex messaging is sorely needed in the broader progressive movement. There is a gender spectrum, a sexuality spectrum in terms of attraction, but also a sex spectrum, a whole beautiful rainbow of intersex conditions too. We range from chimeras—two zygotes that fuse in the womb to create one human with XXXY chromosomes—to someone like me, who started out with XY chromosomes but resisted becoming more masculine-presenting in utero before reaching what was obviously an "optional" finish line. The binary is some bullshit reinforced by doctors who contort reality into more rigid terms that fit into traditional black and white narratives. The world is way more beautiful in color.

As intersex people fight for others to understand the fluidity of gender and sexual preferences, if we aren't fully forgotten, then we are often used to prove a point. Homophobes and TERFs (trans-exclusionary radical feminists) can't refute the spectrum of biological sex when 160 million humans exist who were born not purely male or female in terms of internal gonads and/or external genitalia. For some people, intersex forms are the physical evidence they can't deny; if bodies break the binary, then how could our gender expression or sexual attraction not follow suit, right? But in order to be that tangible, visible proof that every letter of the queer acronym exists (for those who won't simply believe folks are who they say they are), *we* also have to exist. That means our physicality can't be erased by surgeries before we're old enough to say anything about it. If you're going to use us as the crux of your arguments, you gotta fight for us too.

In the meantime, I'm not going to shut up about it. Just because something challenges us, or requires us to reconsider our own arguments and how to talk about our beliefs, doesn't mean we should avoid it. If I might indulge myself in a moment of pettiness . . . some folks, even within the queer community, fight tooth and nail against the extended acronym, insisting that the plus sign in LGBTQ+ includes intersex folks and whoever else they're too lazy to learn about. If that's the case, couldn't we just shorten it to TQIA+? The Q in LGBTQIA+ stands for queer—a term many would argue inherently includes lesbians, gays, and bisexuals, the Ls and the Gs and the Bs. These same folks would be up in arms to fight their own erasure yet are some of the most vocal on Twitter threads claiming that the flag is already inclusive enough and that adding the intersex component in 2021 killed the vibe. It's giving: yes, my grandparents were immigrants but now that *my* family's safe, we gotta close the borders because resources are just too strapped these days.

This is not to say that institutions should start utilizing the full LGBTQIA+ acronym if they aren't committed to our actual inclusion beyond the letter. The moment that inspired me to write these very words you're reading was one of tokenism in one of the most "progressive" cities in our country. While visiting my friend Forest in Portland, Oregon, we ducked into the famous Powell's City of Books. I was initially excited to find not just a "Queer" section but a special area labeled "Trans/Intersex/ Genderqueer." Unfortunately, I could not find one book about intersex folks after scouring every cover in every row; my rush of initial euphoria turned quickly to tears. Spaces touting themselves as bastions of radical inclusion—whether physical places like bookstores or movements and political parties—must keep evolving and stay open to outside forces endeavoring to keep them accountable. Rather than complaining about the problem at customer service that day, though, I decided to write one of the stories that I couldn't find and to ensure that my book is stocked on Powell's shelves.

We have to remain curious enough to continually reexamine our own dogma and courageous enough to change it, when necessary. Back in 2018 I had founded my own firm, Intrepida Strategy, to run Danielle's campaign. Ever the high school Latin nerd, I chose the word "intrepida" on the basis of its two interpretations, depending on how you conjugate it: neuter plural *intrepida* means "bold actions," and feminine singular means "courageous woman." I am now a courageous woman ready to take bold actions on my own terms. I lived twenty-seven years in the closet and spent a few more working within the structures that ultimately keep voices like mine silenced. I am no longer willing to live by anyone else's rules to get ahead nor to allow those too committed to the status quo—on both sides of the aisle and marching within my own Pride parade—to keep me behind.

Once I shook the desire to fit into anyone else's mold, personally and politically, things started to blossom for me. Around this time, Julie Cohen—one of the directors of the film *RBG*—reached out to let me know that Focus Features was on board to produce a documentary, *Every Body*, about my and two other intersex activists' work in the context of the broader intersex movement. She was inspired to document the intersex experience after working with Shana Knizhnik, author of *Notorious R.B.G.* (where the late justice originally gained this moniker) and an intersex activist herself. It is one of my greatest regrets that we weren't able to lift a case regarding medical injustice toward the intersex community while Justice Ginsburg was still alive; given her lifelong commitment to fighting discrimination on the basis of sex, we could have had quite a platform to expand the notion of what sex even means. But having my own work, and that of other activists I admire, highlighted by a director who worked extensively with the iconic justice is pretty great consolation.

Julie's films focus on gender equity and those putting their lives on the line to fight for it, like her most recent movie about former congresswoman and gun rights hero Gabrielle Giffords—*Gabby Giffords Won't Back Down* (2022). Giffords was shot in the head at a community event in Arizona, almost robbing her of her life and severely disrupting her ability to speak, but this didn't stop her. She may not sound the way ableist society would deem "normal" anymore, but she didn't choose to seclude herself in silence; she keeps showing up. Beyond her work on gun policy, I know that inspires many folks like me who've been told we should hide our discrepancy from the norm. I had the honor of attending the premiere and meeting both Giffords and her husband, US senator Mark Kelly. It's weird but humbling to think I'll be at my own premiere soon. I created my own stage, and now it's time to step onto it without fear.

Beyond fancy film events, I'm out here hustling to pay my

bills while trying to create equal opportunity for all human beings. As far as a day job, one of the hats I wear is working as a part-time partner at the Pride Fund—a venture capital firm that invests in and builds an ecosystem for LGBTQIA+ entrepreneurs, especially in states where they face adverse barriers to accessing capital. I also give talks at corporations that want to do better or engage in influencer work that aligns with my goals as an activist, such as a campaign for Parade underwear about feeling comfortable in your own skin.

By night, I work on policy and direct action. As a human rights commissioner for the city of Austin, I've supported legislation that's helped us achieve a variety of policy goals—from the provision of paid sick leave for all Austin workers to the decriminalization of homelessness to comprehensive police reform. In this role, I helped pass a historic ordinance to provide education to the parents and doctors of intersex kids—the first of its kind in the South—though it has since faced hurdles to implementation despite nine votes of support on City Council and just one opposing. The national prevalence of anti-trans and -intersex legislation, with a record number of such bills having been filed in 2023, has chilled even local efforts to do better by these communities. Sometimes progress involves one step forward, three steps back...

Serving as the current vice chair of our city's Human Rights Commission can be a real challenge. Our ability to move the ball forward is often thwarted not just by a national climate that is hostile to civil liberties or attacks by a state that loves to restrict them, but even by our own inability to come together as a governing board. You'd think such a commission in a place like Austin would be more progressive than it is. I've tried to advance additional decriminalization efforts, specifically focused on sex work and psilocybin, only to be thwarted by people who haven't quite caught up to where readers of this book might be. That's government, though. Sometimes you're a bridge builder, and sometimes you're pushing an agenda others aren't ready to hear, let alone support.

Intersex folks are pretty well-suited for that position, I guess, and I remain inspired to stay in this role by the organizer who originally appointed me to it—then Austin City Council member, now US congressperson Greg Casar. It's also important for representation's sake; as far as I know, before Kimberly Zieselman was appointed to the US Department of State, I was the only out intersex government official in our country (a statistic I hope will change soon!). Having the title of Commissioner also lends some weight when I fight the State of Texas, which is a lot—like whenever it tries to ban healthcare for trans kids or when it ultimately succeeded, unfortunately, in restricting all access to abortions.

Whichever hat I happen to be wearing at a given moment, above all, I'm out in these streets trying to thrive and help others survive as intersex people. The biggest brunt of this is raising visibility and increasing representation; as my friend River Gallo often reminds me, we can't change policy to solve our problems if they don't even know we're here. This sometimes involves fun stuff, like attending receptions at the White House or speaking on podcasts with everyone's favorite *Queer Eye* host, Jonathan

Van Ness (sorry to the rest of the Fab Five!), who wrote this book's foreword.

I actually have Trump to thank for originally meeting JVN, oddly enough . . . I live in multifamily housing, and at the time my upstairs neighbors were former Trump Administration execs. When Trump lost his reelection, they had left DC in a huff and headed to Austin, where they proceeded to make loud noises at all hours of the night, often waking me up at 2, 4, and 6 a.m. (not sure what they were doing up there and didn't have the balls [pun intended] to ask!).

One Friday night, I'd gotten home late only to be awoken around 3:30 a.m. by familiar thumps upstairs. I grabbed my phone to send an angry text and somehow got sidetracked onto social media, where I saw a Facebook post advertising a launch event for JVN Hair the next morning. They were doing a pop-up grooming event on the popular Austin thoroughfare on South Congress and—given that I saw this info at an ungodly hour and had plenty of time to ready myself—I was determined to be the first in line. Yes, I wanted my hair done, but I mainly wanted the opportunity to approach this nonbinary goddex in person and see how much they knew about all of the injustice my intersex community faces.

As it turns out, I inadvertently fell back asleep for a sec and only arrived in time to make *second* in line, but once my turn was called, JVN hadn't showed up yet. I patiently let each person behind me get in front of me, remaining in the queue until Jonathan made it to the scene. At that point, I beelined straight to the floor-length-caftaned public figure and told them that I liked their half-up high ponytail but really wanted to know whether they were aware of the surgeries that mutilated little intersex kids motivated, by how their bodies break the binary. You gotta shoot your shot! JVN seemed a bit shocked for sure. Ever living up to the name of their podcast, however (*Getting Curious*), they told me they would love to learn more and referred me to one of their management team members to set up some time to talk.

(At the time, JVN had said something to the effect of "We should chat about it on *Getting Curious*" and, because I wasn't yet aware they had a podcast by that name, I think I said something stupid like "For sure, I'm on Getting Curious all the time"–thinking it was some newfangled app like Clubhouse or TikTok that I'd neglected to download. Perhaps JVN didn't hear that part, or perhaps they were just too gracious to have called me out at the time, but I did end up going on *Getting Curious* with them–kicking off what's become a beautiful friendship. They show up constantly for social justice, and I've tried to support how I can, wrangling meetings with Beto O'Rourke's team during his Texas gubernatorial race to help amplify Beto's campaign on JVN's platform, and tag-teaming on Instagram Live to promote JVN's book *Love That Story*).

I've made videos for social media with other public figures as well–in government, such as Cory Booker, Ilhan Omar, Andrew Gillum, and Pete Buttigieg; and in entertainment, such as former *Twilight* vampire Ashley Greene and even Harry Potter wizard Daniel Radcliffe–to try to get folks' attention. Because we still lack a critical mass of "out" intersex individuals to band together and engage in grass*roots* organizing city by city, as has worked for other movements, we currently have to engage in grass*tops* organizing: getting high-profile individuals to take action in support of our cause.

Once our message has penetrated the masses widely enough, there will be as many visible intersex advocates as there are trans activists—or more, given that we are estimated to account for a larger percentage of the population. The growth of our movement is accelerating, as evidenced by the fact that two other major motion pictures centered on intersex topics premiered at SXSW in the spring of 2023 (*Who I Am Not* and *Bloody Hell*) before ours will even launch at the Tribeca Festival that summer. Walking red carpets now paves the way for us to eventually grab needed seats in halls of power.

Far more often than what audiences will view on big screens, though, my grind involves unseen—and decidedly unsexy—grunt work. Systemic change to better serve our community necessarily involves politics and media advocacy but also requires massive reforms within healthcare. I spend lots of time educating med students, doctors, and medical support staff on how to help intersex folks who've experienced decades of medical trauma—or who hadn't found out they were intersex until later in life after a doctor happened to pore over their medical records for some unrelated health reason.

Beyond sharing stories, I spend an inordinate amount of time acting as a guinea pig for clinics—figuring out which hormones and delivery systems work best for my body. So much of the intersex narrative revolves around childhood surgeries, which makes sense—they're the most jarring example of the health inequities we face, therefore the most compelling stories to recruit empathetic humans formerly ignorant of our plight to our cause. While the prevalence of surgeries is the injustice most shocking to others, though, the utter dearth of competent care for intersex adults is far less talked about but equally dire.

Because so many of us are sterilized in our youth, there is very little research about the long-term needs of intersex bodies left intact. And because there is so little data available on our bodies and how they function, it's hard to generate the political urgency and financial justification for investing in developing better—or even any—standards of care. Just one example of how the absence of best practices leaves us in harm's way:

In my younger years, I took standard birth control as hormone replacement. This included a week of placebos per month, which enables people with wombs to retain their monthly cycle. I've never had a uterus, though, and don't get a period—nor do I have gonads to produce hormones my body needs to function properly, after they were surgically removed. So I suffered one week per month without any needed hormonal inputs into a body that had been forcibly rendered sterile. This, compounded for years on end, exacerbated the endocrine withdrawal that leached calcium from my bones and ultimately left them brittle.

The clinical inequity we face in the healthcare realm is influenced by a variety of factors. Some doctors are heavily biased, like the well-reputed endocrinologist who recently told me "perhaps my bones were weak because God intended them to be" (not even sure what she meant, to be honest—that God was punishing me for being created intersex by his own design?).

Others are simply woefully undereducated. Given that we're absent or, at the very least, severely underrepresented in medical school curricula, we become the experts. As a result of all of this, intersex individuals are largely left to fend for ourselves in the healthcare arena, scraping whatever limited research we can find to direct medical professionals on how to care for our bodies.

I'm currently leading a project for Texas Health Action (THA)—an organization whose Kind Clinics provide sexual heath and wellness for the LGBTQIA+ community across Texas—to help change that. We are creating an intersex healthcare program, which they'll offer alongside the transgender transition support they already provide. This dream project arose from years of dedicated advocacy as a member of their community advisory board, having spent just as long evaluating gaps in how they currently operate, as a frequent patient of their STI testing and gender care arms. I'm proud of this effort I'm leading within this one health system and hope it will serve as a model for others to follow. I'm grateful THA are kind (again, pun intended) enough to make this dream a reality for Texans who need it but we need to vastly expand the scope of this work and replicate it at scale.

Requiring individual patients to serve as squeaky wheels within the medical institutions they frequent for years on end—then to lead large-scale consulting projects with said institutions, in order to rectify care gaps—is entirely unsustainable. Plus, the generalized lack of medical protocols nationwide translates into a lack of insurance reimbursements for our care. While birth control, and even sometimes hormone therapy for trans folks, is often subsidized, the same active drugs are not always covered for our own hormonal regulation. To put this in perspective: because the doctors removed my testes in infancy, I now need hormone replacement therapy to support basic bodily functions and have to pay for these essential meds out of pocket. Not only have we not received reparations for the harm done to our bodies, but we have to foot the bill to resolve the medical issues created by this harm.

While I hope to one day hold society accountable for past harms, much of my energy goes toward preventing ongoing harm in the present. Besides all my work to improve conditions for us inside medical institutions, I also spend more time than I'd like protesting outside some of them. Many hospitals continue to perpetuate irreparable harm on helpless kids—like Weill Cornell Medical College, where my family's tuition dollars have been utilized to keep abusive doctors on staff (and which we'll revisit more extensively later). One day, we'll put policies in place to prevent bad actors from chopping up children; in the meantime, we do what we can to stop the bleeding.

It often feels like an insurmountable burden falls on us intersex activists. Until the rest of the queer and reproductive rights movements—let alone broader society—take up our struggle for body autonomy as part of their own, the few of us who are "out" have quite a bit of work that falls on our only-human shoulders. A lot of this is heavy emotional labor, requiring us to relive our traumas and relay them in a way that's sufficiently shocking to elicit some sort of reaction from our audience and significant enough that they might carry the story with them and help scale our efforts. We keep preening, day after day, like zoo animals, but the cage never disappears.

Maddeningly, intersex activists receive less than 1 percent of all available LGBTQIA+ funding to accomplish our goals, let alone to sustain ourselves. We're moving mountains on shoe-string budgets, most of us on top of full-time jobs. I don't want to rant or stray into boohoo bummer-jams territory, but I also don't want to minimize how desperately drained and direly under-compensated each and every one of us is . . . From the large-scale work of policy change to the micro-level assistance we provide to intersex patients seeking hormone access or parents requesting advice around the world on a daily basis, we vacillate between the role of doctor and politician but without the hefty paychecks. We are pouring constantly into vessels that suck us dry without offering a drop of water in return. We need the world to believe us, and we need them to pay us too.

I learned from watching a documentary on the Jeffrey Ep-stein trials that crimes against children are taken more seriously and warrant heavier sentences than other crimes, so I'm waiting for the world to finally wake up to what's happening to intersex kids. Beyond nonconsensual surgeries, intersex infanticide is still reported in certain parts of Kenya, Uganda, India, China, and other countries; seen as a bad omen, kids born visibly in between the sex binary are killed at birth in many remote rural communities where it takes longer for our messages to reach people. I'm quite certain that if any other class of children was regularly murdered, an alarm bell would be sounded across the globe. Beyond all the work we do as activists, our survival is revolutionary—our very existence is resistance.

Thankfully, slowly but surely people are starting to listen.

Following years of street protests and behind-the-scenes organizing, in 2020 Lurie Children's Hospital in Chicago became the first in the country to end unconsented operations on intersex children. The inclusive Pride Flag was updated to incorporate the intersex flag a year after, and despite significant backlash within the queer community, I've seen a lot of these flags flying in prominent locations around the world—even in the *Sex and the City* reboot. Mainstream TV shows like Samantha Bee's *Full Frontal* have started to incorporate intersex rights into their coverage of the world's ills and what needs to be changed. The Biden Administration even included us in the 2022 Pride Month "Executive Order on Advancing Equality for Lesbian, Gay, Bisexual, Transgender, Queer, and Intersex Individuals," which mandated a report on "promising practices for advancing health equity" for intersex people and a plan to improve it across all branches of government.

I try to relish these wins—to pause and enjoy the fruits of my labor in the moment—because they restore my hope and recharge my energy to continue fighting. I was present at the signing of this historic order, which also happens to be the first time a US president ever said the word "intersex" in a public-facing speech of any type. I was asked to be the cover feature for *Austin Woman* magazine, demonstrating that a more comprehensive idea of what it means to be a woman is coming to light, even in Texas. Plus, it felt really big to see my face in local newsstands when a magazine is what prompted me to discover myself and own my identity in the first place.

On a personal level, when my mom testified at New York's

city council in support of intersex kids, that probably juiced me up for an entire year. People often assume that I followed in my mom's footsteps, and in a certain sense, I did. She graduated from the Wharton School, one of the top global business schools, back in the 1980s when very few women were even admitted. As a groundbreaking woman—making waves in systems not built for me—I channel her, for sure. She didn't become politically engaged until after I became an activist, though. In some ways the apple didn't fall far from the tree; in others, the tree fell on the apple.

Even the smaller victories feel momentous. When I see an organization, an influential individual, or an everyday person using the full LGBTQIA+ acronym or flying the intersex-inclusive Pride Flag, my heart flutters. When a drop-down menu on an online form grasps the difference between sex and gender and doesn't lump intersex with gender identities—so that I'm able to register that I'm both intersex *and* a woman—my heart swells. My heart fully bursts every time a new intersex person comes out to me personally or on social media because it means the work is working! I lift their voices whenever I can (stay tuned for the acknowledgments section—"Pardners"—coming up!) while also replenishing my own stores when I need to. This involves saying *no*, often, to avoid being sucked completely dry. Anything I sink my teeth into now has to feel and taste good; the best peach is a juicy one, after all.

SINTONIZE SUA VIBRAÇÃO

Sintonize sua vibração	*Tune your own vibration*
Não há tempo pra viver em vão	*There's no time to live in vain*
E não pense mais em desistir	*And don't think again about quitting*
Existe um mundo que só quer te ver sorrir	*There's a world that just wants to see you smile*

NATIRUTS

siptoplize sha vibração

So you've made it through more than three decades of my life. Congrats—I know it's been a doozy. There's so much more I could have included. I'll always have epic times with friends to look back on—road-tripping through Morocco or across Hungary and Romania, wandering deep into the jungles of Colombia and Panama, training with Olympic rowers in Spain, and dancing in the rain till sunrise on the beaches of the Dominican Republic. I also relish many simple yet equally meaningful moments on the sofa with my dog, where this reformed party girl turned early bird now spends the vast majority of her evenings. The journey I've brought y'all along on, though, is rooted in those instances when I struggled to, and then finally managed to, love myself as an intersex person; I hope it might teach y'all how to love people like me better, in the way we've always deserved.

The path I've taken to get here may not make a lot of sense to anyone besides me, but one thing I'm sure we can all agree upon is that I've always set my own vibe. *Tune your own vibration* is a lyric from one of my favorite Brazilian samba-reggae bands, arguably their most iconic song. Beyond tuning my own vibration, I've dedicated my life to raising everyone's vibes as high as I'm able. I've reached the point of self-love where I feel blessed to have been born in a way that grants me the opportunity to elevate our collective consciousness and conscience. Y'all have the privilege to help amplify our calls for better.

If there's one thing I hope everyone who reads this book walks away with, intersex or not, it's this: I urge each of y'all to tune your own vibration too, rather than living in vain by trying to ride someone else's frequency. I got this musical phrase tattooed on my leg, the script morphing into a sound wave, to remind myself of the power of being myself—even on days when I inevitably struggle with self-worth, as we all do sometimes. It's fitting that the lyric is situated on my inner thigh because we all know by this point that quite a few musicians have been up in that spot. I'm bringing intersexy back. And I actually have a vase on the mantel above my fireplace filled with potpourri and quite a few drumsticks—my equivalent of a trophy case, showcasing a history of Inter-sexual Healing. I'll let you interpret that how you will . . .

Flexing on my romantic conquests aside, I think there's a reason I've always gravitated toward musicians. Artists and activists are kindred spirits. We motivate crowds and push the boundaries on what's socially acceptable. We share pieces of ourselves most others wouldn't dare to, to help make the world brighter and help others feel less alone. I know I'll be doing that till the day I die and am grateful to have picked up friends along the way who do the same—from musicians like Steve Aoki, Matias Aguayo, and the members of Brazilian psychedelic rock band Boogarins to many activists across a variety of intersectional movements. I'm going to shout out a few of them here in the hopes that you learn a bit in the process and support their work beyond these pages. After nine chapters on my past, consider this one a blueprint for a better future—a pathway to move past allyship and toward becoming a real accomplice who can compel others to do the same.

The cool thing about the intersex movement is that it's not a monolith. We show up in many ways to shed light on who we are and what we need from a broad spectrum of perspectives. In the Focus Features documentary *Every Body*, I'm lucky to share the screen with two of our most illustrious leaders, River Gallo and Sean Saifa Wall. River is a nonbinary, Latinx actor and model who has graced everything from LinkedIn and Crocs commercials to a short film they also directed called *Ponyboi*. They're bringing intersex representation to the entertainment industry where it's sorely needed, understanding that we won't be able to effect any political change if we can't change hearts and minds first. River's cheekbones could cut diamonds and their laugh is infectious. They are a beam of light in my life and the world at large. I highly recommend following them on Instagram and watching any project they put out.

Saifa is a Black, intersex activist and force of nature—one of the originators in the movement and a fierce fighter for Black liberation too. Currently getting his doctoral degree in the UK, Saifa has made more media appearances than I can count and is a strong proponent for direct action. In August 2021 we tag-teamed on organizing a rally at Weill Cornell Medical College—alongside everyone from New York state senators to Cecilia Gentili from the iconic TV show *Pose*—to protest the continued employment of Dr. Dix Poppas. Despite years of our pleading for him to change his ways, Poppas continues to engage in what the United Nations Committee Against Torture defines as intersex genital mutilation, or IGM.

People think of genital mutilation as happening only to tribal women of the African Horn, but young people suffer it across the US daily. IGM is the nonconsensual and medically unnecessary practice that forces aesthetic surgeries onto intersex children's genitalia. This includes cutting down little kids' clitorises to what certain doctors deem to be a "normal" size. According to a 2010 Hastings Center paper called "Bad Vibrations," Poppas used vibrators on these children to gauge how much sensation remained after his "work." Besides being perverted and disgusting, this is a documented example of modern-day eugenics. As intersex activist Kiran Foster said so eloquently, "Intersex issues do not stand on their own, but rather highlight the way medical science is founded upon the white supremacist urge to pathologize and mutilate the bodies and cultures of people who do not fit their worldview."

The Hastings Center—the world's oldest independent, nonpartisan, interdisciplinary research institute on bioethics—puts IGM into a broader context, lest we forget that modern gynecology was founded upon experiments on enslaved women's bodies. Per "Bad Vibrations":

> *In "The Rhetoric of Dehumanization: An Analysis of Medical Reports of the Tuskegee Syphilis Project," Martha Solomon brilliantly demonstrates how the project's researchers hid their work in plain sight. Specifically, Solomon used the published reports of the Tuskegee syphilis study—which involved medical professionals actively withholding medicines from black men with syphilis for four decades—to show how the dehumanizing, scientized language of modern medicine "can obscure and deemphasize any ethical, nonscientific perspective."*

We have been dehumanized to benefit the experimental whims of those who seek to force our conformity to a white, cisheteropatriarchal norm. When I first mentioned intersex kids being treated like lab rats, I was not exaggerating. The physical and psychological "results" of these "clinical trials" are devastating.

These surgeries are also often used to push an intersex kid's genitals one way or another, to better fit a false binary that society is more comfortable with. Usually, doctors default to creating a vagina, because, as some have said, "it's easier to dig a hole than to build a pole." Sometimes doctors make the wrong choice with often irreversible surgeries, leaving intersex kids trapped in anatomy they never asked for or leading them to transition later in life. Even if some intersex people's gender ends up aligning with the outcome of surgeries forced upon them, is the "reward" worth the risk?

At our rallies, we chant "change their hearts, not our parts" because a body shouldn't have to be forcibly altered to fit a predetermined box on a piece of paper when, in fact, birth certificates could be changed to fit the reality of human bodies. We host these rallies in major cities to raise visibility of what's happening in view of as many people as possible and in earshot of major media outlets that might carry our words even farther, but we lift the voices of intersex folks everywhere—including rural areas where the disparities are most pronounced.

Living close to a major city like Philadelphia in my youth, my family had at least some access to doctors who knew how to treat my body. My care wasn't always free of bias and never focused on affirming—rather than masking—who I was. At the very least I didn't have to travel far distances to be seen. That changed when I moved elsewhere and had to fly back to the Northeast to receive care, at great personal expense. This is a luxury that most intersex people and their families can't afford, and shouldn't have to, but it was worth it to me to continue seeing a doctor who could somewhat meet my needs.

The doctor I saw since early adolescence happened to move from Philadelphia to New York City to work at Weill Cornell Medicine around the time I went to Cornell University farther upstate. When I eventually came out and started advocating for the needs of my community, and against her colleague Dr. Poppas, this doctor I'd seen for a decade stopped talking to me altogether. Since then, I've been unable to find intersex-competent gynecologists or endocrinologists in Texas and have been left high and dry. Medical neglect has led to lifelong harm, including a recent diagnosis of osteoporosis—at age thirty-two rather than sixty-two, as you might expect—because insufficient hormone therapy has been leaching calcium from my bones for years.

Brittle bones are not an uncommon result of medical malpractice. Others have had to sacrifice much more at the hands of doctors perpetrating IGM, like the integrity of their genitalia and the outward expression of their gender identity. I'm grateful that Saifa has led the charge in protesting so many bad actors in the US, including at Lurie Children's Hospital of Chicago—which, as we have seen, became the first medical institution in the United States to denounce and further investigate intersex genital surgeries on infants. This caused a domino effect that led to public hospital systems for entire cities, such as NYC Health + Hospitals, to follow suit. Unfortunately, private hospitals like Weill Cornell aren't covered under this mandate, so we'll keep applying pressure until they change. I'm grateful for all the Columbia med students who've also taken up our fight, risking their future careers to protest at NewYork-Presbyterian, where Poppas is also employed.

These unrelenting efforts are thanks to the leadership of Intersex Justice Project, an organization lifting up the work of intersex people of color co-founded by Saifa and Pidgeon Pagonis. As Susanna Barkataki, a yoga instructor of Indian descent, explains: "To be colonized is to become a stranger in your own land, your own body, your own experience." Saifa and Pidgeon have worked for years both to tie intersex surgeries into narratives of broader colonizer violence and to decolonize the intersex activist space. The movement not only has been historically white-led but also has centered the voices of those trapped in the oppressive idea that we are simply disordered men or women, rather than something else altogether—different but whole in our own right.

Just like how being gay isn't a disorder, being intersex is a naturally occurring phenomenon. Although the world is still coming around to that idea, we have dramatically reduced the instance of "electroshock therapy" on gay kids in the past few decades alone. As nonconsensual surgeries on intersex kids are also conversion therapy, using scalpels instead of psychiatrists, I have hope—I know—that we can put a stop to them too. We just have to take that first step, by helping people understand that being intersex isn't a pathology, it's our identity. We have to assume that identity, proudly. Being intersex is my identity. And it's beautiful.

Intersex is beautiful. Trans is beautiful. That's why I am an advocate for trans rights too. We come with a range of physical traits, but as people who have faced and continue to face discrimination for our discrepancy from the gender norm, we all have certain things in common. We've all experienced shame and stigma. We've all faced uncertainty about the best way to care for our health and well-being due to the lack of proper medical care and resources. We've all faced questions about who we are. Whereas trans people are killed or barred from public spaces for existing as who they are, intersex people are chopped up as children and forced to cope with little to no resources on how to do so. But whether through bathrooms or surgeries, we all share that experience of being shoved into, or pushed out of, a box in which we don't fit. That perspective binds us, through empathy.

Empathy is learning an aspect of someone else's humanity, not because you've necessarily shared or experienced it yourself, but because you're open to understanding it. Empathy is a choice, not a circumstance one is born into; we should recognize how powerful that is. We need labels now—the LGBTQIA+ acronym, races, genders, nationalities—because we have to demand improvement of specific issues that all of these specific communities face. But the more we can cross those barriers through radical empathy, the better chance we *all* have together.

This is why we need inclusivity and intersectionality—not for a reason of tokenism, but because we never know whether one person's perspective will be that one cog in the gear that makes the light bulb go off for someone else in a new way. It's why I chose to advocate against the Texas bathroom bill in the first place. That legislation wouldn't have affected me, but perhaps my words opened the mind of someone on that committee who wasn't hearing the cries of who *would* be affected: my trans brothers, sisters, and comrades. I didn't say "this isn't my fight." I admitted the privilege of my circumstance, as a cis-passing white woman, and asked to join the fight for people I cared about. And what was my added value? One new perspective, from one more lived experience, that might plant a seed that one day blossoms into compassion.

I chose empathy and I chose bravery. People think courage is a personality trait, but it's actually a choice we all are capable of making. It is the choice to move forward with something difficult, regardless of circumstances and fear—to put a foot forward, rather than to stay still. Choice is the most necessary, and powerful, thing that exists. It is the difference between life as a free agent and as a slave to circumstance. That's why I fight human trafficking but support voluntary sex work. That's why I support reproductive rights, more specifically, unbarred access to safe and affordable abortions. That's why we cannot enact medically unnecessary surgeries on young intersex bodies before we've had the agency to determine who we are.

For all of us who have chosen to break some sort of societal expectation rooted in patriarchal conditioning, our greatest "threat" to "normalcy" is also our greatest strength. Those of us who have broken some sort of binary—trans people, bisexual people, intersex people who claim our identity openly—we are the least understood but actually the most powerful. We transcend the boxes that limit our potential, which gives us more perspective. We aren't bound by the circumstances everyone else blindly accepts, so we are innately more innovative. We refuse to settle for a reductive set of options, so we become more resourceful. And we've all had to go against the grain to claim our identity, so we're resilient AF too.

Although trans and intersex kids are often demonized in today's world, it wasn't always that way. We are not unholy; targeting us is. We deserve to grow up sacred, not scared. In many precolonial cultures, we were revered, rather than persecuted. Across the globe, various indigenous groups believed that sitting on the border between sexes—in that liminal space—not only gave us a better understanding of the human experience but made us more attuned to other realms too, beyond thresholds others can't always see.

In Borneo, we were considered intermediaries between heaven and earth, uniting the feminine element of earth and the masculine element of heaven in one person. (I had a similar reading from my Colombian shaman when Amaru, a serpent-like deity, passed through me during my *yagé* ritual in the jungle. My guide told me this spirit is reputed for breaking all boundaries between masculine and feminine, the realm of the skies and that of the earth, and chose to inhabit me out of all the other attendees of our retreat precisely because I am intersex.) Many Native Americans believed—some still do—we weren't a broken version of one sex; instead, we were doubly blessed with a combination of both spirits. In these cultures and others, we were valued as healers, seers, teachers.

My first boyfriend, Mike, whom I've reconnected with and become close to again in recent years, helped me understand that we're still inherently gifted as superconnectors. When I came out to him, many years after we broke up, something clicked for him—a more practical than spiritual explanation for why we're hyperattuned:

> *That explains a lot… you've always been able to forge some sort of connection with any type of person, whether it be a sex worker experiencing homelessness in South Africa or an oil-funded Republican in the Texas Legislature. I think that growing up never knowing anyone like yourself, you found ways to detect some sort of commonality with anyone you came in contact with, as a way to relate. What started as a survival mechanism has become your greatest strength. You can always unearth and latch onto even the most latent kernel of someone else's humanity; now you're using it to help others understand your own.*

When you consider all this, you might realize that intersex people are a natural fit for leadership in the fight for our collective liberation. There are even records of an intersex person playing a major role in the American Revolution—Polish general Casimir Pulaski, who led a charge that forced the British to retreat at a pivotal instance during the Battle of Brandywine, a stone's throw from where I grew up. In 2019 results of studies on his exhumed remains determined Pulaski may have been intersex—experts positing that he most likely had the variation called congenital adrenal hyperplasia (CAH). In a 2019 article in *Smithsonian Magazine* titled "Was the Revolutionary War Hero Casimir Pulaski Intersex?," author Brigit Katz wrote: "In light of the new evidence, Pulaski can be seen as a valiant representative of a group that has largely been erased from the historical record—not only through omission, but also through deliberate attempts to shoehorn intersex individuals into one gender or another." It is significant because it shows we were there and part of a defining moment in our nation's history and the fabric of American culture.

We actually weren't always erased from positions of prominence either. Acceptance of intersex folks was the norm in many societies for millennia, as evidenced in ancient Roman and Greek mythology and even recorded lineages of Egyptian pharaohs. Many have heard of the Egyptian queen Nefertiti, but far fewer know that her spouse, Akhenaten, was intersex. As Sabeau Rea wrote in "LGBTime Machine: Ancient Rome," posted online in 2017 by the National Organization for Women, "What makes Akhenaten's sex so spectacular is how universally *unspectacular* it was to the Ancient Egyptians. While the Pharaoh's policies, including the implementation of monotheistic worship of the sun god, were *incredibly* badly received, their sex and gender were never criticized, or even questioned. In fact, their physicality was so widely accepted that most official renderings of the pharaoh were depicted true-to-form." I guess not *all* intersex folks can be gifted leaders... turns out there are Caitlyn Jenners in any century.

Beyond mere acceptance of intersex bodies, appreciation for our beautiful manifestation of humanity endures even in some modern religions like Hinduism and Judaism. One story in Genesis in the Hebrew Bible (the "Old Testament") about the creation of human beings can be translated as: "And God created the human being in God's image. **God created it in the image of God; male and female,** God created them" (Gen 1:27). In this reading, the original being was male *and* female; God created *them*—as in the singular nonbinary pronoun. Another story (Gen 2:21-22) says that God removed a rib from Adam to make Eve, implying that women owe men for our creation, but there is another interpretation, paraphrased from Mark Sameth's article in the *Forward* entitled "Was Adam A Hermaphrodite?": In Exodus 26:20, the same word, צלע, the word that has traditionally been understood to mean "rib" is used to mean "side"—it was a construction term referring to the side or the wall of the Tabernacle. So, if we understand that the phrase should mean "And God took the side of the Human . . . ," all of a sudden, things start to make a bit more sense, and reminiscent of Plato's Symposium, even: the original human being was both male and female, with multiple sides, and God split them in half.

People forget that the Bible was originally written in Hebrew, and many things have been lost in translation over the years, sometimes being intentionally manipulated to serve the personal worldviews of interpreters. Yes, many religions and the societies that embrace them negate our holiness (see the Vatican's official proclamation on trans and intersex folks in recent years . . .); others, however, see us as divine—the original human being whence all others came.

Religion and science go hand in hand in that regard: as we've already seen, all humans start out with a common genital anatomy until seven weeks after conception, when they sexually differentiate. Seven days of creation, seven weeks postconception . . . tomato tomahto. Whether you're more into religious texts or biology text-books, *these* are the interpretations I choose to subscribe to. We've always been here, we're blessed to be here, and we deserve to be worshiped, dammit! (Or loved and respected, at the very least.)

I've leaned more heavily into Judaism in recent years, in light of learning about this interpretation as well as my own Jewish ancestry on my mom's side (the Roth name could have tipped you off). I grew up with primarily Jewish friends and joined them at Hebrew School weekly—so I didn't feel left out, though it was usually the last place they wanted to be—and even sometimes led prayers at Seders and Shabbat dinners. Both of my exes are Jewish, and when I discovered my Ashkenazi heritage in recent years, they both relished informing their parents that they hadn't been dating a *shiksa* after all. I bring this up in light of rising anti-Semitism in this country, feeling it extra important to claim this community and affirm my commitment to them. I encourage anyone to follow Adam Eli and Abby Chava Stein for strong Jewish leadership within the LGBTQIA+ community—at the very least in order to understand how these stigmatized yet beautiful identities can support one another with grace.

Whether you're intersex or not and regardless of your religious beliefs, the more we fully own who we are—the parts we've been told to hide or suppress or be ashamed of—the more permission we give others to do the same. So many of us have been robbed of control over our own bodies—whether through slut-shaming that detracts from our pleasure, rape that violates our consent, surgery that negates our autonomy, or restricted access to abortion that limits our future. The first thing we need to do is realize that the shame we hold surrounding these issues is not ours, it's *theirs*; weighing us down with it keeps us exactly where they want us and prevents our flight to freedom. The first step to releasing it is talking about it, to reduce the stigma that isolates us and prevents us from collectively demanding better.

Loneliness is corrosive; the antidote is community. That's the thing: None of us is alone, though it may feel that way sometimes. In the queer community, we fly rainbow flags as beacons to remind one another of that fact—to symbolize the beautiful spectrum of our existence. But it's gonna take a lot more than raising a multicolored piece of cloth or typing a virtual emoji version to make it safe, let alone "normal," to exist as who we are everywhere and at all times. We each have to keep showing up for one another—in a variety of ways, in a variety of environments—even when it feels uncomfortable or outright scary to do so.

My work at the Pride Fund helps create a business environment where LGBTQIA+ entrepreneurs can show up as their *full* selves, even in places like Texas. My work as Human Rights Commissioner helps fight a political environment that oppresses those trying to show up as their *best* selves—whether by getting an abortion, to avoid having a kid they can't afford as they pursue their dreams and contribute to society, or by participating on a sports team to build personal self-worth and collective morale (intersex bodies are proof that the outdated binary used to categorize athletes is insufficient to fit reality—but I digress . . .). My work as a *very small scale* influencer is to keep showing up as my most *authentic* self—affirming to my followers that posting captions about compact and connected urban policy *and* ass shots on the same Instagram feed doesn't make someone a professional liability, it makes them a human being.

This isn't to say that I have it all figured out or that I'm everyone's cup of tea. If you've noticed, my authenticity tends to manifest as radical honesty in any and all circumstances. Maybe because I'm from Philly or because I was forced to wear a facade for so long, I'd rather just call it how it is. I speak truth to power, even when that power is held by people I consider friends or family. Sometimes that involves losing them in the process; sometimes it involves some really uncomfortable confrontations with my own mirror.

Hurricane Alicia occasionally leaves destruction in her wake . . . as Danielle aptly put it: "A hurricane causes damage, but we become more resilient having gone through it." I think if we were to collectively decide that real respect is just as much about candor as it is about manners, society would be a lot stronger. We need more Thanksgiving table discussions with racist family members 365. As of now, this approach earns trust but doesn't necessarily make you popular—especially in southern cultures. Not everyone who's met me would say I'm nice, but I hope they'd admit I'm earnest.

Perhaps this explains why I've achieved a lot professionally but still sometimes struggle with the personal. Dating, in particular, as an out intersex woman can be rough. When you spend your days exposing your childhood trauma to the world as an activist, it can be tough to dredge up any last dregs of vulnerability for the dating circuit—especially when, at one point or another, you'll have to lay yourself bare in explaining a very unfamiliar existence to your date too. When that process leads to rejection in your most defenseless state, it's hard not to build up walls. Of course, it's easier to remember the ones who didn't want you than all the ones who did; I am grateful for each and every sexual and romantic experience that made me feel seen and wanted, even loved. There are many of those, even if I don't include the vast majority of them here, out of a desire to protect their privacy and my own. (There are parts of my life I deserve to keep for myself and cherish without sharing too.)

There have been instances, though, when people have made advances rooted in a fetishized interest in seeing "what it looks like down there." Usually, I can filter out the pervs, but sometimes when I'm in bed with someone, it suddenly becomes clear that that person is less interested in me and more in experimenting with what it's like to fuck an intersex person. I have also run into men who have initiated sexual contact but then needed me to persuade them that I'm in fact not a man—or to reassure them that their heterosexuality is not threatened by being with me. Interrogation is *not* foreplay. Talk about killing the mood...

What happens most frequently, though, is someone abandoning me once they figure out who I really am. I'll meet someone at a bar or on an app who's attracted to me off the bat but then that person discovers—after a cursory internet search or after I mention something about my work—that I'm intersex, and bounces. I can never be certain whether this is because they feel threatened by the idea of being with someone who's as public as I am or because they can't deal with the internalized homophobia or transphobia that dating someone like me triggers in them. It's a bit different from being immediately excluded from someone's dating options on the basis of visible reasons, based in racism or fatphobia, because it gives me the chance to initially get my hopes up before getting let down.

You'd think I'd be numb to it at this point, and I have developed a callous edge, taking much longer to open up to new prospects and sometimes suppressing the butterflies before they have a chance to take flight. But it still hurts every time. I know these aren't people I'm meant to end up with, but each time this happens it dredges up the age-old wondering if maybe I really *am* unlovable for who I am. It validates my parents' and doctors' original fears that I'd end up alone if people found out I was intersex—or so my inner child tells me, whose wounded anxiety I still heed too much on occasions. But I am a grown woman now, and I have the ability to remind myself otherwise.

I remind myself that I'm surrounded by people who love me. I remind myself that the day will come when I meet that one person who chooses to love me above anyone else. I remind myself that it's not just waiting for someone to choose me, *I* have agency in that matter too. Very little of my life trajectory is "standard," so I shouldn't expect my path to life partnership to be standard either. I've made many choices to get me to this point, and they've been *mine*, not those of whatever person I happen to be comparing myself to in the moment, robbing me of my joy. For the days I forget these things, I've tacked to the fridge the contents of a fortune cookie I once had: "Nothing is more difficult, and therefore more precious, than to be able to decide."

Yes, I went to a bougie college where all my friends graduated to be doctors, lawyers, or bankers (power to them!). I went a very different direction, away from stability but toward meaning, and I have rarely since had a neat and tidy answer to the most common question we get in a capitalist society: "What do you do?" Choosing a vocation over a career has meant opting for a payoff in changed systems—probably long after I'll be alive to benefit from them—rather than in my bank account. It entails declining many of the weddings and bachelorette parties I'm invited to in order to invest in life events that bring me closer to my goals—ones you don't necessarily send out "save-the-dates" for. It involves becoming a person who is less easily understood at family gatherings and is perceived as a less viable candidate on dating apps—someone who doesn't make a lot of sense on paper or to anyone besides myself, most of the time.

The "babies" I bring into the world aren't cuddly and cute and often force people to reckon with sides of themselves they might not be ready to look at (like this book!). The most important relationship in my life is with my vision, intuition, and purpose. It is my own life and I wouldn't choose any other. It is exhausting yet gratifying; difficult yet precious. I write this to remind anyone, intersex or not, who is taking a less traditional path why you chose it—to let you know that I respect your choices, even if I can't always see or comprehend them. I celebrate you by celebrating myself, with or without a gift registry.

Perhaps I'm still single because I love myself first and am waiting for someone who won't ask me to sacrifice that. I'm making up for all the lost time I sought that love somewhere outside of myself, not even really believing I was worthy of it. While I may not have found myself in a long-term relationship since coming out, that time on my own has given me space to find myself. It's given me time to understand who I really am versus who I'd always been told I should be, and to understand and build unwavering confidence in my true worth.

I know I'm not single because I'm intersex; I'm single because I'm a vibe and I'm patiently awaiting someone who can match or, even better, raise it. I know plenty of intersex folks in loving relationships, and I know one day I'll find one that sticks—with someone who loves me *because* of who I am, not in spite of it. Plus, I refuse to lead a life driven by fear; I'd rather opt toward faith.

I have faith that one day intersex people will be so normalized in society that we won't have to worry about the danger of "disclosing" who we are leading to rejection or threats to our physical safety. I have faith that eventually society will recognize that we aren't freaks and are in fact super hot. I have faith that in the meantime, I'll find someone who not only loves me but wants to partner with me in building this reality. I'll keep tuning my vibration until I find someone who sings in the same key. (Bad Bunny, perhaps?) Together we'll leave the safety of this urban center to live on a ranch somewhere in the Hill Country outside of Austin. There, we'll continue to break down barriers of acceptance in rural areas—along with having a bunch of goats and chickens and maybe even a dog rescue called the Chihuahua Ranch, where I can enjoy the rest of my days in the peace all intersex people deserve.

The greatest irony I've found, living intersex in Texas and

frequenting both gay bars and honky-tonks, is that the cultures of being queer and being Texan are actually one and the same: both are based in defiant grit, surviving against all odds. Both are built on self-determination and not letting others define who you are. Both are steeped in deep, often aggressive to the point of being comical, pride. Once the rest of Texas understands that our existence isn't a threat to theirs and that—swapping out a star for a rainbow, or some platform heels for spurred boots—it's really not all that different from theirs either, we'll all be a lot healthier and happier. "Y'all" is the perfect gender-neutral word, after all.

The Bullock Texas State History Museum's website emphasizes the importance of the frontier in our state's foundation, pointing out that "new ideas, new jobs, new identities, new starts and new money were all possible on the vast frontier." What may seem like a new identity to some has actually been around for all of human existence; intersex folks are on the frontier of male and female, and instead of fearing what that unknown means, we should consider that it might just be a great place to live. Black and white is boring—we should embrace the gray areas. The coolest shit in life exists on the border, at the boundary, or in that messy gray space.

Texas was born from conflict, winning independence from Mexico in 1836; in this current fight, we're just asking for that same liberty to declare who we are on our own terms. To let freedom ring, you must let us be. From the big domed building out East on Capitol Hill to our own pink granite State Capitol here in Austin, my message is the same: Intersex kids should be left intact, not pruned to fit someone else's paradigm. Even Lady Bird Johnson knew the best flowers are the ones left wild. It's time for this inverse cowgirl to ride off into a field of purple bluebonnets and yellow roses, the hues of my beloved intersex flag. I hope you'll join me!

AFTERWORD
(WELCOME)

Let a teacher wave away the flies
and put a plaster on the wound.

Don't turn your head. Keep looking at
the bandaged place. That's where the
light enters you.

—RUMI, FROM "CHILDHOOD FRIENDS"
(TRANS. COLEMAN BARKS)

welcome

I commemorated the completion of this book with one more tattoo: Welcome. Seems like a weird one to get at the end of something, right? Writing this book was difficult for me—baring my
soul, including past traumas and transgressions, for a bunch
of strangers to read. The process was almost like a prolonged
therapy session covering my whole life, over the course of mere

months, and knowing the transcripts would be public domain. It was hard, but it was also healing. I interspersed long writing sessions with trail runs, giving myself a break to move my body while soaking in some fresh air and the Texas sun.

On one of those writing breaks, I took a wrong step on Slaughter Creek Trail and skidded into a rock. The fall flayed open my left knee—fitting to the trail's name—which was already addled with scars from past falls. It also left an excruciatingly painful abrasion burn, similar to road rash, covering a good portion of the shin. Bleeding profusely and unable to run, I hobbled the three miles back to my car and drove to an urgent care center. The doctor told me I wouldn't be able to run for weeks, and even once I had healed, the wounds were profound enough that I should expect severe scarring. I fell into a deep funk.

During those weeks, though, I met myself the most deeply. Unable to run from the dark parts of my past as I unearthed them to embed into these pages, I faced my whole self for the first time. And even once I was able to run again, my left leg looked entirely different from how it had before. Rather than lamenting this, I decided to lean into it. I came across an oft-quoted line attributed to Persian poet Rumi (see Rumi's words in the epigraph) that spoke to me as it has to others: "The wound is the place where the light enters you"—and it's true. All the ugly, painful things I've experienced have wounded and scarred me for sure but also have taught me some of the biggest lessons about myself and the world around me. Once I healed sufficiently, I tattooed a one-word mantra—inspired by this quote—on my wounded knee.

Now carrying a final, permanent mark *on* my body, I realized there was heaviness *in* it I no longer wanted to bear. It was at this time I booked my *yagé* ceremony, having heard that only by facing my demons would I finally be able to rid myself of them. After a multiday journey into the Amazon, I found myself without electricity or running water but with a greater connection to my truest nature than I'd ever felt before. In the sacred *maloka* structure where this same native lineage had conducted this same ritual for over five hundred years, I cleansed past traumas from my cells and gained divine insight into my future. It wasn't easy . . . the medicinal liquid I drank into my body caused most other liquids to leave it. In each heave of vomit or bout of diarrhea, though, I ejected my resentment toward doctors and family members or expelled my lingering belief that I would never be worthy of real love. I had to confront some of my heaviest spiritual "baggage" in order to shed it, and as I purged what was no longer serving me, I made space for better.

In the jungle, the person I had come to be died and I was reborn; it wasn't a "new me," it was the me I'd always been before absorbing thirty-two years of society telling me how I should think or feel. The experience was key to my salvation because I realized that while I *can't* accelerate the pathway to freedom for all intersex people, I *could* liberate myself from the experiences that had been weighing me down and slowing my own trajectory toward it. And unburdening ourselves of all of the shame, stigma, and other encumbrances that keep us from loving ourselves and others *is* enlightenment.

I left my limiting beliefs behind, in pools of waste that absorbed into the roots of the trees that sheltered me during the hardest parts of my ceremony. And life has blossomed for me since! Professionally, I've planted the seeds of more competent healthcare for intersex adults through the creation of the intersex care offering that will launch in Kind Clinics across Texas in the summer of 2023. Personally, I've found myself in the springtime of a new love that's still in its sapling stage but has the potential to help me grow taller and stronger than I ever thought possible.

I hope that this book might inspire some of y'all to revisit your own wounds and learn from them. It's scary to do so and not always pleasant. You might find yourself cold and weak—vomiting on the wet, hard ground of lands that feel foreign and overwhelming, as I did in the Amazon. Or maybe the process will trip you up, rip you open even more deeply than where you started, draw blood and leave you struggling to recognize yourself—as I felt after my fall on the trail. But it's only once we address what's harmed us, or how we've harmed ourselves, that we have the opportunity to reclaim what was taken.

Acknowledging our scars is more fruitful than spending our lives trying to hide them. So rather than wearing pants for the rest of my days after I fell, I got a tattoo amidst the scar tissue that might draw even more attention to it. Rather than finding the right foundation to cover my now heavily marred knee, I chose to commemorate it as a portal to future lessons. Rather than obscuring past pain, I chose to beckon the light in. From these scars to the inevitable future ones to follow: Welcome.

PARDNERS

No inverse cowgirl rides alone.

In a world where we're often left out entirely, here I'm including intersex folks first. There are so many people for me to thank and for y'all to learn from. Beyond River and Saifa from the documentary *Every Body* and a few others interspersed throughout these pages, many other intersex activists inspire me and are worthy of commendation (and compensation). Pidgeon Pagonis is one of my biggest intersex heroes and has a book out that I hope you'll read as well, titled *Nobody Needs to Know: A Memoir* (2023). They've evolved a lot across many phases of their work, in terms of both their gender expression and the approaches they use and spaces in which they operate, but they've been in it to win it for quite some time.

Pidgeon was at the White House with me for the signing of President Biden's Pride Month Executive Order, as was Kimberly Zieselman. Kimberly, aka KZ, is the former head of inter-ACT—a central intersex advocacy organization that serves as a great jumping-off point for aspiring activists and allies and has a medical advisory board to support doctors and hospitals as well. KZ also has a book out titled *XOXY: A Memoir* (2020) and currently serves as a US State Department senior policy advisor to the Special Envoy to Advance the Human Rights of Lesbian, Gay, Bisexual, Transgender, Queer, and Intersex (LGBTQI+) Persons. Her appointment is the first instance of out intersex representation at the federal government level in the history of our country; it's about damn time.

On the policy front, Scout Silverstein has been killing it too. They work at the intersection of intersex justice and eating disorder recovery—which is vital, given the body image issues that our community struggles with in a variety of permutations. Scout also led the charge on the ban on intersex surgeries in New York City public hospitals and is working on implementing one statewide. Entire countries have enacted such bans, but the efforts here in a nation as large as the United States are more piecemeal; we tried in California and will keep pushing. Both Hans Lindahl and Bria King were lynchpins in the California push and are consistent drivers of the movement at large. Jahni Leggett and Jenn Levine are fierce favorites, whom I miss dearly. And I'm grateful to see new leaders such as Lia, Courtney, Justin, Alyssa, Val,

Tatenda, Alice, Marisa, Jubilee, Jessica, and so many more rising through the ranks.

This list doesn't include the movement leaders outside of the US—from the activists in the thriving South African intersex movement like Crystal, Sharon, and Dimakatso, to Hiker in China and Irene in Russia—and is by no means complete. Plus, those of us currently agitating owe everything to early organizers like members of the Intersex Society of North America, who first gathered twenty years before I even came out; the documentary *Every Body* pays homage to them better than I have in these pages. Although I hope someone eventually writes a comprehensive history of the intersex movement or How to Support the Intersex Movement 101, this ain't it. This is my story, which I hope will help folks understand the need for more books like it and the ones I have mentioned.

My role in this work isn't drafting an intersex encyclopedia (perhaps a project for one of our intersex academics like Georgiann Davis?); it's being a coalition builder. As an organizer tied into political systems at all levels and the broader progressive movement at large, I'm devoted to getting our demands included in policy platforms and Democratic infrastructure. As a white, cis-passing woman, I'm focused on getting folks who find my aesthetic more personally relatable to listen to and learn from others—regardless of their party affiliation.

I hope such individuals are highlighting or sticky-noting the names of the people and organizations I've mentioned in order to follow them on social media or subscribe to their listservs later. Because when it comes to allies, the ones who've traditionally showed up hardest are those who have the most on their plates already. My best co-conspirators have always been people of color and trans folks—the ones who know what it's like to be excluded from other movements led by those who hold more privilege in the comparative spectrum, like white women or gays.

I am in awe of the leadership of southern Black-led organizations like Austin Justice Coalition, What's in the Mirror?, and Embrace Austin, and I am humbled that they've always found ways to lift me up through their work, despite the color of my skin. They also know what it's like to have to fight "science" that strips whole people of their rights on the basis of natural physical characteristics—from the racist phrenology historically used to justify slavery to whatever cherry-picked statistics the Right uses to negate the need for critical race theory in schools. They too understand that many of the healthcare inequities Black women face—struggling to have their pain believed by doctors and to access competent care most Americans take for granted—resemble the same barriers we're trying to dismantle.

I am also awestruck by trans and nonbinary activists in my corner—Angel Flores, Alok Vaid-Menon, and of course JVN—who include in their mantle our fight to get necessary hormonal care covered by insurance companies or to be recognized in census data. (Speaking of, a recent Pew poll posits that approximately 5 percent of young adults in the US now identify as trans or gender diverse; I'm convinced that once our own visibility increases and data collection measures improve, the intersex percentage of the population will skyrocket far beyond 2 percent.)

High-profile trans voices are key to amplifying our work but so are the on-the-ground organizers. Rocky, Emmett, Ash, Adri, Andrea, and everyone leading the Transgender Education Network of Texas fight tirelessly alongside me in the trenches at the State Capitol, sometimes sleeping on the hard marble floors and testifying at all hours of the night for months on end. Speaking of trenches, my friend Jamie Hash and her partner, Emily, helped overturn the trans military ban from the inside; I hope we might one day overturn the intersex military ban too.

Besides trans activists, reproductive rights organizers are hands down the most relentless advocates for the well-being of *all* of us here in Texas. I'm grateful to Amanda, formerly of the Lilith Fund, and Rockie, formerly of the Frontera Fund, who were early adopters of a more inclusive platform for body autonomy—asserting that true reproductive justice must include intersex justice. I'm indebted too to my southern progressive politico friends, who put in the often unsexy yet necessary elbow grease to run orgs and manage campaigns: Malenie, Jen, Saurah, Mary, Meebs, and more are building the bench for a more just future in which we have much cuter and more representative butts in government seats.

I'm especially thankful for the support of organizations and people committed to fostering LGBTQIA+ wellness in the face of those hell-bent on doing us harm. InterConnect and interACT do so much for the intersex community specifically (special shout-outs to Alesdair, Sylvan, and Marissa). Then there are the groups improving queer healthcare more broadly that lead the way as "early adopters" of intersex inclusion: Out Youth, Texas Health Action and its Kind Clinics, and Central Health all listened to me and endeavored to do better "before it was cool." Med student Casey Orozco-Poore and researcher Kyle Knight from Human Rights Watch also deserve special shout-outs as the most committed accomplices in the medical arena I know.

Then there's all the family who commit to *my* LGBTQIA+ wellness, whether it be watching my puppy when I need a break or taking my late-night phone calls when I need to unload: my chosen family, like AJ, Jules, Emily, Tanisha, Forest, Tim, Melissa, Kaitlin, Taylor, Lauren—who makes and sells sparkly Figa amulets to wear around your neck, in case you don't want to get one tattooed onto yours like I did, at www.FigaJewelry.com—and so many others. Plus the friends who've stuck with me since the early days of this roller coaster: Anjali, Meghan, Artemis, Julia, Jenny, Jess, the list goes on (and I hope no one will be too upset if they've been left out . . . I'm blessed to have a lot of friends—less blessed with a mind that's quick to forget faces and names, even of those I love very much).

My bio family has also given me so much and put up with a lot in the process. My brother, Max, has always supported me, even though I wasn't always the nicest to him while we were growing up. My mom has always thrown herself full force behind the people and things she loves. She's also one of the smartest and most conscientious people I know. I like to think I've inherited all of this from her. I know I've inherited my dad's goofy sense of humor. And all else aside, he has worked hard to provide us with opportunities others don't have, which has enabled me to become the activist I am.

Although I know how tough life is for intersex people, it's real rough on our parents too; I'd be remiss if I didn't acknowledge that. For all of our collective flaws, I'm grateful that mine have joined me on this rocky journey of self-discovery and haven't hopped off the ride yet. They never chose to be public figures, and I appreciate that the disruption of their privacy is neither fun nor easy. Maybe one day they'll understand that sometimes the shield of privacy can keep us locked in problematic patterns or outdated ways of being that would benefit from exposure to the light of the world outside. Regardless, I hope they know their sacrifice helps many others feel seen and understood for the first time.

If you haven't felt that way while reading this book, I can empathize. It's what inspired me to write it in the first place ... maybe it's time you write one too. If you're intersex: we need way more intersex narratives published to help fill that shelf at Powell's City of Books and all bookstores. If you're endosex (a weird term to refer to those who aren't intersex—I'll let *y'all* feel like the odd ones for once!), there are plenty of identities whose stories haven't even begun to surface yet. It's about time we heard them; yippee ki-yay, y'all! Let this literary journey be the kick in the pants you need to kick down that stable door and hop in the saddle yourself. I'll end with the queerest, and cheesiest, words of encouragement you could expect in a gender-expansive cowboy saga: Ride 'em, cow-them!